ACTION

Right No 2 Soho Square, 1983, Wolf Suschitzky.

ACTION!

Fifty Years in the Life of a Union

QUOTE FROM
TERENCE DONOVAN

"A team of very professional ex-film men who worked with me at the Paris Fashion collection under circumstances which made the Notting Hill Gate riots seem like a holiday camp.

At no point did they flinch.

Also a wonderfully pleasant place in which to edit. The drive to Sutton is just about right to de-rev the brain before starting work".

Thank you Terence!

Quadrant Television Ltd.

SURREY HOUSE · SUTTON · SURREY SM1 4QQ
TELEPHONE: 01-642 0924 · TELEX: 946564 BISPRS G

CONTENTS

In addition to our contributors and the staff at ACTT's offices in Soho Square, the editors would like to thank the following individuals for their special help in preparing ACTION!

Arts International, BBC, Doreen Burt, Jack Breckon, Christopher Brunel, Capital Radio, Channel 4, Mike Cohen, Sid Cole, Eric Cross, Michael Crossley, Thorold Dickinson, Drummond Drury, John Dyble, Mark Ellidge, John Ellis of Large Door/Spectre, George and Peggy Elvin, EVTR, Don Fisher, Muriel Gardiner, Nancy Garner, Kay Gladstone of the Imperial War Museum, Arthur Graham, Granada Television, Sheila Gray, Ernie Greenwood, Mick Hartney, Ted Lloyd, Lynda Lookes, Jean Macdonald, Pat Mantle, Norman Martlew, Alan McNeal, Alan Messer, Ivor Montagu, The Morning Star, Jacqui Mulder, National Film Archive, National Video Corporation, Beverly Neill, Ogilvy & Mather, Chris Pereira, Sudhi Pradhan, George Rains, Rank Film Laboratories, Eric Richards, Ken Roberts, John Rose, David Samuelson, Saatchi & Saatchi, Syd Shelton, Brian Shemmings, Marilyn Stafford, Wolf Suschitzky, Talbot Television, Joe Telford, Thames Television, J. Walter Thompson, Roy Thompson, University of Stirling, Fred Varley, Andrew Wiard, Brian Worth, Yorkshire Post, Yorkshire Television.

ACTT would like to thank the following advertisers for their support in the preparation of ACTION!

Abacus Productions, AKA Film Services, Alpha Films, Anglia Television, Anvil Film & Recording Group, Any Effects, Artifax, Nigel Ashcroft Associates, Geoff Axtell Associates, BBH/P & E, BFI, Border Television, Robert Bosch, Brent Walker Film Distributors, Brian Stevens Animated Films, Broadcast, Broadcast Facilities International, Bruton Music, BTS Video, Buck Film Laboratories, Bushey Studios, CAL Video Graphics, Capital Radio, Carlton Television, Central Independent Television, Ceta Video, Channel 4 Television, Channel Television, Cine-Europe and Cine-Video, Cinexsa Film Productions, The Commercial Unit, Contemporary Films, The Creative Partnership, Crosswind Films, Crystal Film & Video, CTS Studios, CTVC, Steve Dann Associates, Direct Effects, Eejay Caterers, 88 Film Productions, Enumerator Films, Eothen Films, Euston Films, EVTR, Ewart Television, Eyeline Film & Video, Five Cities Films, FTS (Freight Forwarders), Godman Hurst Productions, Goldcrest, Hugh Gordon, Grampian Television, Granada Television, Greendow, The Guild Organisation, Hadmor Productions, Stewart Hardy Films, HTV, ICP Films, Image Transfer, IPPA, ITN, Kadek Vision, Kay Film & Video, Kemps Film & Television Yearbook, Kodak, The Ladd Company, Lansdowne Recording Studios, Lazer Films, Limehouse Productions, London Films, London Weekend Television, Lynx Video, Malachite, Mercury Studio Sound, Metro Goldwyn Mayer/United Artists, The Mighty Movie Company, Molinare, Adrian Munsey Productions, MVP Media Video Productions, National Film & Television School, Pinewood Studios, Platypus, Portman Productions, Provideo, Pye TVT, Quadrant Television, Rank Film Distributors, Ravensdale Film & Television, Rediffusion, Salon Productions, The Samuelson Group, SVC Sanderson Vere Crane, Scottish Television, Secker Walker Partnership, Shootsey, Sidhartha Films, Sony Broadcast, Soundcraft Network Video, Spectre Productions, Spectrum Video & Film Production Services, The Robert Stigwood Organisation, Tarn, Technicolor Ltd, Tele-Cine, Television South West, Television Weekly, Televisual, Thames Television, Third Eye Productions, Thorn EMI Elstree Studios, The Townhouse, Trade Films, The Travel Company, Trilion, TV-am, TVS, Twickenham Film Studios, TWTV, Tyburn Productions, Tyne Tees Television, Ulster Television, Universal Pictures, Vernon Hiles, Vernon Howe Films, Video Arts, Video Connection (Films), Visnews, Richard Williams Animation, John Wood Studios, Yorkshire Television.

ACTION! celebrates in words and pictures the achievements of a trade union and its members during 50 momentous years.

With the help of many ACTT members, staff and former staff, the editors have tried to trace the highlights of a half century that has seen the transformation of the film and broadcasting industries.

This book is a tribute, rather than a history. We hope that the thousands who are not mentioned in its pages will recognise something of themselves and their aspirations in the story that we and the contributors tell.

Peter Avis

Edited, Designed, Photographed and Produced by John Andow, Peter Avis, Roland Blunk, Sue Hayes, Gary King, Margaret Mulvihill, Christopher Oldroyd, Lynn Sowerby.

The opinions expressed in this book are those of the contributors and not necessarily those of the publishers. We cannot accept responsibility for any errors or omissions.

FOREWORD

On behalf of the TUC I would like to extend hearty congratulations to the Association of Cinematograph, Television and allied Technicians on reaching its 50th anniversary.

As a young lad, I thrilled to the spills of Saturday morning pictures with the best of them. Today at the flick of a switch we can be transported into the middle of great events, political debates or variety spectaculars, while relaxing in our own homes. It is all too easy to forget how much the magical world of cinema and television depends on the hard work and dedication of people who are never seen in front of the cameras. The cinema has been with us almost a century, and ACTT is almost as old as broadcasting itself. Yet it is astonishing to think of the immense technological leaps made between silent black-and-white films at the turn of the century and the wondrous special effects of modern-day films; from the old crystal radio set to microchip hardware and satellite broadcasting.

It is a mark of ACTT's strength and adaptability that despite these tremendous and fast-paced developments the union is not only keeping pace but is often ahead of the industry in its ideas and planning. While seeking to represent and defend its members' interests with zeal and determination, ACTT has never lost sight of what the future can bring. Video, cable and stereo television in particular are in their

infancy and it is
clear that broadcasting is on the
brink of a new era. These developments can be
used for ill or good. ACTT is in the forefront of
the campaign to ensure that these are used for
the maximum social benefit and not just to line
the pockets of a few - for education and
enlightenment rather that exploitation.

   With ACTT and other broadcasting unions
working together we can view the future with
confidence. I wish ACTT prosperity for the
next 50 years.

Lionel Murray, General Secretary, TUC

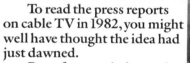

To read the press reports on cable TV in 1982, you might well have thought the idea had just dawned.

But of course, it dawned long ago: for Rediffusion, in 1936. That's when we installed our first cable TV system.

Since 1947, we've had a Research and Development Department working solely on cable TV networks all over the world.

In the 1950's we brought TV (by cable, of course) to Hong Kong. That system, in its day, became the biggest cable TV network in the world, for which we also produced the entire programming (in English and Chinese).

In 1952 we put in a system serving 58,000 homes in Montreal, which was then the biggest cable network in North America.

As far back as 1969 we patented a 'new' switched cable TV system and, in the following year, initiated its first public trial on a network at Dennisport, Massachusetts.

By 1976 we had installed the first fibre optic TV trunk cable at Hastings.

In 1978, in Arnhem, we were

FOR US, CABLE TV DAWNED LONG AGO

the first to use optic fibre in final distribution and, what's more, with full multi-channel switched systems.

No company in the world has been researching cable TV so long or holds so many of the patents involved. Our total now stands at 139 with five more patents pending.

But cable distribution is far from being our only involvement in television.

We have designed, constructed, equipped and operated television studios, outside broadcast units and closed circuit TV systems.

We have taken radio and television broadcasting to many other countries.

We were instrumental (with our B.E.T. parent) in establishing Independent Television in the U.K.

Remember Associated-Rediffusion?

We have more experience than most of producing radio and television programming in many languages.

We manufacture TV sets, in addition to being one of the leading TV and video rental companies.

We are also the second largest, British-owned computer company.

So we are uniquely placed, not only to understand the relationship between television and cable, but also to apply advanced computer technology in developing the all important interactive capabilities of our new cable system.

Not surprisingly, if it had been left to us, cable TV would not have been so long arriving in Britain.

But, thanks to the years of patient preparation, it will be all the better for the delay.

REDIFFUSION, CARLTON HOUSE, LOWER REGENT STREET, LONDON SW1Y 4LS.

1933
A UNION IS BORN

What happened when Stan Jolly met Captain Cope — and young George Elvin talked to Lord Asquith's son.

In 1933 the Association of Cine-Technicians was born. A boom was beginning in films, but few of the benefits of rapidly rising production came to British film technicians. In the labs, hours were long and overtime excessive — not always paid for — and pay was generally low. Conditions were no better in the studios, where periods of frenetic activity alternated with slackness and unemployment. Hours were seldom less than ten a day, and there were many occasions, lasting weeks at a time, when the staff did not get home at all. In addition, British film workers felt that they were the poor relations in their own industry. Though foreign talent had been important, and indeed welcome, in the very early days of British films, by 1933 the terms 'ace technician' and foreign technician were too synonymous for comfort. In the year that ACT was

Above ACT's birth certificate. The organisation was now a union.
Right A top-hat technician. Frank Bassill, for many years senior cameraman at Pathé Gazette, seen in action at the Empire Exhibition, Wembley, in 1924. He was made an Honorary Member of the union in 1949.

9

Ivor Montagu

Ivor Montagu, film-maker, author, peace campaigner, one-time Foreign Editor of the *Daily Worker* and former President of the International Table Tennis Federation, is one of the most colourful pioneer members of the union. This is how the *Cine-Technician* described him in 1936.

'Burly, untidy, black-haired, overcoated, Ivor Montagu is 32. Younger son of Swaythling family - famous Jewish bankers. Would make good banker himself had he not taken up zoology, table tennis, films and politics. Won medal at age of four, as youngest infant at time to swim length at Bath Club. Educated Westminster, where he studied zoology at South Kensington. Later studied under Lance Hogben at Royal College of Surgeons. Then King's College, Cambridge. Failed on most exams, but was given BA standard for zoology. Finally took degrees in English and French, two terms before his proper time. Had to stay at Cambridge to prove diligence. Found lectures sent him to sleep, so was permitted to do original research. Forgot original research until last week of term. Spent last week measuring skulls of beavers to one hundredth of a millimeter. Original research passed as OK. Took up table tennis because he thought he was good at it - better than anyone else. Found he wasn't, but all the same remained Chairman of International Advisory Council of Table Tennis. Went out to look for mice in Caucasus and thence to films.'

formed, for example, Alexander Korda made his masterpiece, *The Private Life of Henry VIII*. But apart from its stars, its subject and the fact that it had been made near London, *Henry VIII's* settings,

photography, music and direction were done by foreign film technicians. These circumstances stimulated talk of an 'association'. The first union whisperings began at Gaumont-British Studios in Shepherd's Bush, and soon concerned individuals were gathering in the pubs and restaurants (or rather cafes) of Soho, then as now the heartland of the film industry.

The main union caucus was based at GB and it was the Bush men (no women were involved in those embryonic days) who enlisted the services of Captain Cope, whom Stan Jolly, a sound technician at Shepherd's Bush, had met up with in the local market, to liaise with groups and individuals on behalf of the conception of a union for film technicians. As a result of Cope's travels from studio to studio and the activity of other founder members, the first General Meeting was held in the Blackamoor's Head in Whitcombe Street in May 1933.

With the help of experienced sympathisers from other unions involved

with film workers, Tom O'Brien of the National Association of Theatrical and Kine Employees and Alfred Wall of Equity (previously of the London Trades Council), rules for the organisation were drawn up and recruitment continued. The naive enthusiasm of those very early days was reflected in the decision taken at that first meeting to raise the entrance fee from half-a-crown to ten guineas after the 11th of June so as to induce all possible members to join fast at the bargain rate. Needless to say, two days later the proposed fee of ten guineas was reduced to five - at this stage few decisions were destined to crystalise into hard features of the union's policy. Union it became, however, despite the hopes of some members for a professional body or 'guild' of some kind, because registration as a trade union in June 1933 not only insured the members against the danger of being

prosecuted as a conspiracy, but also satisfied the hopes of the majority of the founding activists for their organisation. Many film technicians did rush to join - it has been estimated that Captain Cope had up to 1,200 members in his book by the end of the year - but many of them lapsed or dropped out altogether when they saw no immediate benefit in the form of a swollen pay packet.

Left Charles Laughton dressed as King Henry VIII and Adolf Hitler dressed for a murderous career.

Left Gainsborough 'boys'. In 1928 Gainsborough was absorbed into the Gaumont-British Picture Corporation. Its small 2-stage studio at Islington served as GB's production arm, while the Bush studios underwent renovation (1928-32) — but it was the Shepherd's Bush technicians who were initiators of the union.

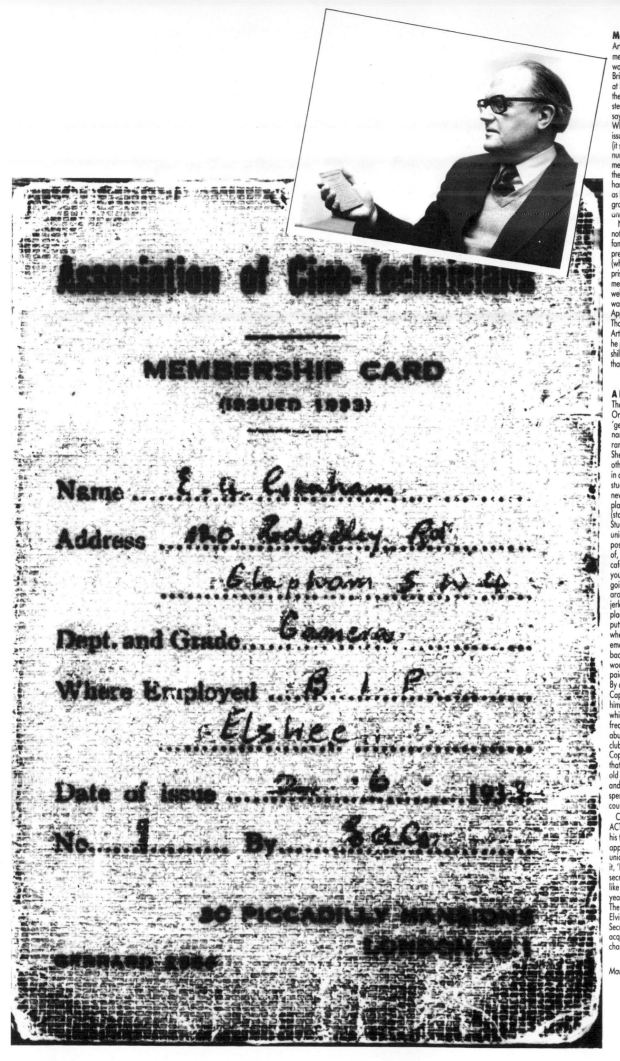

Association of Cine-Technicians

MEMBERSHIP CARD

(ISSUED 1933)

Name .... E. A. Graham ....

Address .... 110 Rodgeley Rd ....
.... Clapham S W 4 ....

Dept. and Grade .... Camera ....

Where Employed .... B.I.P. ....
.... Elstree ....

Date of Issue .... 2nd 6th 1933 ....

No. .... 1 .... By .... S.G. ....

50 PICCADILLY MANSIONS
LONDON W.1

Member number 1

Arthur Graham attended the first big meeting at the Blackamoor's Head. He was then a camera assistant at the British International Studios (now EMI) at Elstree, and he agreed to take on the role of 'studio secretary' (shop steward) for ACT there, simply, he says, because no one else volunteered. When the first membership cards were issued to him for distribution at Elstree (it seems that the second batch, eg number 61 onwards, went to the Bush members), he decided to give himself the number one card, hoping, but hardly expecting, that it would remain as his number in a union that was to grow in strength and celebrate its 50th anniversary in 1903.

Needless to say, however, his card is not Arthur Graham's only claim to fame within the union. Throughout the pre-war years, and again after the war (which he spent a good deal of as a prisoner in Germany), he was a member of the General Council, as well as the Camera Committee after it was formed, and later he sat on the Appeals Committee for several years. Though rather battered and faded, Arthur's original card still records that he paid £2.1.6 (two pounds one shilling and sixpence) in subs during that first year.

A Bloke Named Cope

The infant ACT's first Secretary and Organiser was an energetic 'gentleman' of the officer class named Mathew Cope. Captain Cope ran a 'health and strength' cafe in the Shepherd's Bush Market and, unlike other ACT founder members, he was in a position to venture forth from studio to studio collecting subs from new members. In addition, a small placard bearing the initials ASW (standing for the Association of Studio Workers), which was the union's acronym until the more positive sounding ACT was thought of, was hung up at the back of his cafe. If you were a technician and you had heard of the mysterious goings-on at GB and in various pubs around Soho, you entered this cafe, jerked your head towards the placard while at the same time putting half-a-crown on the table, whereupon the proprietor would emerge and lead you around to the back of the cafe where your name would be entered in a book as a fully paid-up member of the organisation. By all accounts, the monocled Captain Cope 'had quite a way with him' and in his recruitment mission, at which he was very successful, he was frequently thrown out of places and abused. The pioneer members clubbed together to buy Captain Cope a Morris Oxford for £12, so that he could recruit more easily. This old machine frequently broke down, and the Secretary and Organiser spent many a night sleeping in country lanes.

Captain Cope's role in the early ACT was important, but he came to his task with an 'old school-tie approach' rather than that of a trade unionist. As one pioneer member put it, 'He would have been better as the secretary of a golf club or something like that'. Very late in that formative year of '33 Captain Cope resigned. The way was then clear for George Elvin to come in as the first General Secretary, and Captain Cope then acquired the status of a legendary character from the earliest days.

Margaret Mulvihill

Above Jack Noble with the unmistakable Ken Gordon, 'a large, rotund, cherubic-faced individual'.

When 25-year-old George Elvin came on the scene on the recommendation of his brother Harold in 1934, less than a quarter of the 80-odd members remaining were fully paid-up and three months' rent was owed on the top floor room in Piccadilly Mansions (overlooking the Circus) that served as ACT's headquarters. To get George, as the first General Secretary, past the liftman, Thorold Dickinson took a fiver from his wallet. Nine or so of the other pioneer activists also volunteered to be personally responsible for George's pay and the office running costs until things got going properly.

Two Gainsborough pictures in the making. **Top Right** *Jack's the Boy.* **Below** *Friday the 13th.*

The real beginning

George Elvin's arrival did mark a turning point, the real beginning of ACT's history as a fighting organisation. From then on, meetings were real meetings and interest among lapsed members revived as new ones were recruited. George set himself two immediate priorities - the

establishment of a journal and an employment bureau for members, so that members could enjoy some immediate benefits - and he had realised them by 1935. Even so, things were pretty precarious. Desmond Dickinson, then frequently an out-of-work cameraman, used to subsist by the income he derived from the pin tables he installed in various studios. George and Bunny Garner, who was now assisting George in the office, used to give him half his patrol money when he did his rounds on Fridays, so that Bunny could accompany him and collect subs at the same time. Sometimes they came back without enough money even to split costs with Desmond Dickinson.

In 1937 Anthony Asquith, a distinguished director who had joined ACT in 1934, was first elected as the union's President, a role he fulfilled with great energy and commitment until his death in 1968. But negotiating on behalf of the members was difficult at a time when there were no employers' federations - studios had to be tackled one by one and employers were frequently elusive. The great need was to reach an agreement before an individual producer finished his film, or, as so frequently happened, before he went bust. Between 1925 and 1936 more than 640 film

13

The revolution that swept George to power

It all began with Harold Elvin. At the time he was bicycling around Britain and Europe between jobs, and the Film Society took to paying him to go to the pictures, refunding the cost of the ticket stubs whenever he came back and reporting to me on the films he had seen. One time after making his report, as he was on the doorstep unchaining his bicycle, I asked about his prospects. He said they could be worse and I told him ACT was looking for a secretary. Harold then said, 'What about my brother George, who has the right background, might be interested and is only working part-time for the British Workers' Sports Association?'. I said, 'Bring him round', and Harold did. I called in Neill-Brown, another rebellious committee member (rebellious, that is, against the Cope 'gentlemen's association' syndrome), and we took to George on first sight. We decided to stage a palace revolution at the next committee meeting, which used to take place upstairs in a Wardour Street pub.

In a couple of days there was a regular committee meeting and Neill and I stoked up beforehand. Then we weighed in, and statement by statement, we demolished the secretary (Cope). After about 90 feature-length minutes, the secretary admitted defeat and offered his resignation. Thereupon a large number of the committee said, 'Well I hope you two know what you are doing. Perhaps, you'd better become joint secretaries, honorary'. The committee agreed and Neill and I accepted. We announced that the next meeting of the committee would take place in the same pub in 48 hours' time. When asked why, we said we proposed to offer them a new full-time secretary if we could find one. Then I told George to be in the saloon bar at the hour of the meeting. He didn't have long to wait. The committee was so relieved to lose the previous load (we really had nothing to lose but our chains), that they all said, 'OK, have him up and let's see what he's like'. And George came, was seen and conquered.

What a piece of casting! When ACT got George Elvin for three pounds a week in 1934, it got a bargain.

Thorold Dickinson

companies were registered but no more than three per cent of these were still in business by 1937. Many of them never completed a picture, and many more never completed a second film. The union was anxious to ensure that producers operating with new companies could not start a new film if they owed wages to

their staff on previous productions.

An early dispute at RKO Radio Pictures in Denham in 1939 was precipitated by this thorny issue. It was settled when RKO agreed to pay the members scheduled to work on a new film the wages owing to them from a previous production, which had involved the same producer - in fact the money was deducted from his fee.

ACT's task was an uphill one. All the studios and production companies, with the notable exception of Gaumont-British, refused to negotiate with the upstart union, which found itself with a growing membership whose conditions of work and whose pay were still deteriorating. Eventually, the problem of the elusive employer was alleviated when the Film Group of the Federation of British Industries, though precluded by its constitution from negotiating on labour matters, nevertheless agreed to meet ACT in the form of George Elvin and Sidney Cole. So much for cordial meetings, however. It still required a stern strike threat from laboratory workers (the lab branch had been set up in 1936) at the time of George VI's Coronation before real progress could be made. It was 1939 when the first collective all-industry agreement was signed, thanks to the strength and solidarity of the lab workers. Not long after this, however, the Film Employers' Federation disintegrated, and then separate ones emerged for the principal sections of the industry - the British Film Producers Association for features producers, the Association of Short Film Producers, the Association of Film Laboratory Employers and the Newsreel Association. Then, at last, it was possible to develop effective strategies.

Parallel with such struggles for improved pay and conditions, the union kept a vigilant eye on developments within the crisis-ridden film industry as a whole. The union was concerned, and would continue to be so, about the impact of the 'Hollywood invasion'. The members were painfully aware of the shortcomings of the well-meaning but woefully inadequate and ill-applied 1927 Cinematograph Films Act. This gave rise to the infamous 'quota quickies', by virtue of its requirement that film renters and film exhibitors had to book and show a percentage of British films, rising from the low starting level of five per cent to 20 per cent in 1935. This modest quota did a great deal of harm because producers began to make 'pound a foot' quickies to fulfil it - low budget slapdash films about gangsters and murders with a scratch team of actors and actresses, no rehearsals and, inevitably, an overworked and demoralised crew. These worthless films, which passed as 'British' for the purposes of the Act, were often shown when cinema cleaners were preparing the premises for

Left Young George Elvin — a bargain at three pounds a week.

READING. FROM LEFT TO RIGHT, & FROM TOP TO BOTTOM: MR. KEN. GORDON & MR. G.H. ELVIN.

Land 3):

Above 'Film without a Hero'. Low's interpretation of the quota battle of 1938.
Below 'Variety at the Victoria Palace'. George Elvin, George Hicks (TUC), Tom O'Brien (NATKE) and Anthony Asquith do their thing in the quota battle.

Prater Violet
In his novel, *Prater Violet* (Methuen, 1946) Christopher Isherwood introduces a British film company called Imperial Bulldog, which is said to have been based on Gaumont-British Studios at Shepherd's Bush. Isherwood's description of Imperial Bulldog's premises is especially interesting as a distillation of the film-making scene at the time of ACT's birth. 'Imperial Bulldog had what was probably the oldest studio-site in London. It dated back to early silent days, when directors yelled through megaphones to make themselves heard above the carpenters' hammerings; and great flocks of dazed, deafened, limping, hungry extras were driven hither and thither by aggressive young assistant directors, who barked at them like sheep-dogs. At the time of the panic, when Sound first came to England, and nobody's job was safe, Bulldog had carried through a hasty and rather hysterical reconstruction programme. The whole place was torn down and rebuilt at top speed, most of it as cheaply as possible. No one knew what was coming next: Taste, perhaps, or Smell, or Stereoscopy, or some device that climbed right down out of the screen and ran around in the audience. Nothing seemed impossible, and, in the interim, it was unwise to spend much money on equipment which might be obsolete within a year. The result of the rebuilding was a maze of crooked stairways, claustrophobic passages, abrupt dangerous ramps and Alice in Wonderland doors. Most of the smaller rooms were overcrowded, under-ventilated, separated only by plywood partitions and lit by naked bulbs hanging from wires. Everything was provisional, and liable to electrocute you, fall on your head, or come apart in your hand. "Our motto", said Lawrence Dwight, is, "If it breaks, it's Bulldog".'

the real audiences for the real films - ambitious and prestigious 'supers' from the USA.

When ACT discovered that a new quota Bill was going into committee at the House of Commons, it began a magnificent campaign to bring the members' interests to bear on the proposed legislation. Tom Williams, an ex-miner and a Labour MP, took up the issue on ACT's behalf, while George Elvin and Anthony Asquith mobilised the members for a mass lobby of Parliament. Incidentally, both the General Secretary and the President were able to avail themselves of their respective family political traditions and experience at conjunctures like this. (George Elvin's father, H H Elvin, was then the esteemed Chairman of the TUC, and he provided advice gained from years of experience as a trade unionist and an activist in the labour movement to his son, who, like himself, had started off his career as the extremely young General Secretary of an extremely young union. In a much more informal way, Anthony Asquith's formidable mother, Margot, often put her role as an hostess to the political Establishment at the union's disposal). All the members were informed of the campaign and they turned up at Westminster in strength, pouring into the committee room in the Commons, and cramming the stairs leading to it, so that the committee members were unable to get in. Having registered their concern, the members then marched up Whitehall to a meeting in the Strand, where the next

stage in the campaign was worked out - a campaign that was vital to the survival of the British film industry.

As a result of their work, the quota provisions were extended to short films - previously they had applied only to features - and a minimum cost clause was introduced to kill the shabby tokenism of the old quota quickies. Of particular, and immense long-term, importance, however, was the insertion into the 1938 Cinematograph Act of a fair wages clause. Ironically, this crucial clause, actually got into the Act via the efforts of Lord Strabolgi in the House of Lords. It meant that to qualify as a British film under the new Act, productions had to honour trade union (ie ACT) standards on conditions and pay. The fair wages clause persuaded many hitherto reluctant employers to recognise ACT and to negotiate agreements. In 1938, the union, by then 1,289 members strong, was a permanent and a vigorous element of the film-making landscape of Britain.

1939
ACT GOES TO WAR

Elvin and Asquith kept the studios open, and ACT cameramen recorded brave and terrible deeds of war. Those who worked for victory hoped to build a more just world in peace.

Upon the outbreak of war in 1939, the government came out with a bald announcement to the effect that the Cinematograph Act was to be suspended, and British film production was to cease. And cease it did. Not only were studio technicians affected, but also laboratory employees – and although it seemed likely that some official films would be made, nothing was certain. Accordingly, the first few months of the war became one long trail of ACT officials with, of course, officials from other alarmed bodies, such as NATKE, ETU and the employers, in a united protest against this drastic decision. During the campaign ACT members marched around clutching their cardboard gasmask holders (some members were reputedly using them as sandwich-holders) in protest!

Below Wartime cameramen. Mike Lewis (right) was dropped at Arnhem, captured, but managed to escape.

20

Right 'D-Day Take 1 or Shall I Mark it Now' — Jonah Jones of the Crown Film Unit's Impressions of D-Day.

A newsreeler at Dunkirk

This is an extract from newsreel cameraman Charles Martin's account of the evacuation of Dunkirk in June 1940. He was on a war assignment for Pathé, and was the only cameraman to cover the event at close quarters. He wrote of the experience in the August 1940 issue of *The Cine-Technician*.

'We arrived off Dunkirk in the very early hours of the morning and in the distance could be seen fires and a great pall of smoke. I tried filming this, but unfortunately the light was not strong enough. All during the night the enemy were bombing the towns around this area, and the fore-shore, where our troops were waiting to be taken off, was being constantly shelled. Our poor old ship (an old Clyde paddle-steamer) was shaking from end to end, and I wasn't feeling too steady myself either. When dawn came, I saw thousands of troops standing at the water's edge waiting for us to take them off. All around us were warships and craft of every shape and size waiting to evacuate the troops. I started to take some pictures, but again, unfortunately, on development of the negative, the light proved not strong enough, as this was about 5am. All the material was shot on a Newman Sinclair, the same that I had used on the battle fronts in France. (Incidentally, it was the only camera I was able to bring back - we lost all our other equipment and film, including several thousand feet of negative stock). After taking a number of pictures, I had a very busy and hectic two hours helping the crew get the men aboard. We pulled them up over the side of the ship by ropes as fast as we could, and threw lifebelts to those who had to wait their turn. We then drew away for about half a mile from shore, and took count of how many we had (approximately 400).... We were sending them down below to get what warmth they could, when we heard the noise of approaching aircraft. Within a few seconds, out of the sky came droves of German machines power-diving in all directions and machine-gunning the ships and the troops on the fore-shore. I was on the bridge at the time and was fortunate enough to get a shot of the German aircraft appproaching with our anti-aircraft shells bursting all around it. But I'm afraid that the public won't see any dramatic pictures of them starting to make their dive on our ship; I ducked down and flattened myself out as best I could, while they sprayed the ship with tracer bullets.... When I was able very cautiously to poke my head over the side of the bridge, I saw an amazing sight. A few seconds previously, I'd seen tens of thousands of men standing on the shore; when I looked again the whole beach was like a place of dead men. At the same time as German machines had power-dived on us, three others in quick succession had machine-gunned the beach. The whole mass of troops had thrown themselves flat down on the ground. I waited, and much to my relief saw them stand up again. Only just here and there a few figures remained on the sand. The skipper, finding we could still take some more men, decided to run on to the beach again.... I was fortunate enough to bring back pictures out of all this chaos and turmoil. Ships of all shapes and sizes, fully laden with our troops going back to England; burning Dunkirk with its great pall of smoke; in the foreground some of our ships which had been sunk in this effort of rescue; our men wading or swimming out to us and being hauled aboard; and on the trip back the same men, so shortly after their rescue, once more bright and cheerful. My one great regret is that my early dawn pictures were unsuccessful and that I couldn't bring back with me more material to show what every man jack of them had to endure.'

George Elvin has a vivid memory of meeting Lord Beaverbrook with Anthony Asquith in an effort to persuade him that filmwork should be part of the general war effort. Elvin and Asquith succeeded in gaining the influential peer's support and this move, together with other protests, persuaded the government that a working film industry would be useful, not to say vital, for victory. From then on, ACT found itself in the surprising, though very welcome position of having a boom on its hands due to its new status.

ACT's employment bureau became recognised by the Ministry of Labour as the official vetting body for war-time film technicians - whose work was now deemed to be a 'reserved occupation', a classification initially applied to people of thirty and over with skills and experience that were considered to be indispensable and whose practitioners were therefore refused entry into HM Forces or full-time employment in the Civil Defence Services. (The employment bureau became so established that when one especially conscientious member attempted to get himself registered at a local labour exchange as an unemployed film editor, he was put under a category headed 'ratcatchers and others' - so rare had film workers become in the labour exchanges).

Technicians now queued up to join ACT, the only body with the authority to categorise them as a reserved occupation.

Right A photograph from H J W Currey's album *From El Alamein to the Alps* — an AFPU cine cameraman's record of the war.

George Elvin sat on the appointments board for Service film units and he managed to negotiate a rank for ACT members, with clapper boys being unofficially but effectively deemed privates, cameramen as captains, directors as majors and so on. This sort of understanding made ACT an exceptional trade union during the war in so far as it maintained its own structures within the Services. Also, by dint of making ACT meetings happen on Sunday mornings, members attached to Service film units were excused church parade in order to attend them. Naturally enough,

attendance was very high during the war.

The number of feature films made in Britain did fall during the war, from more than 100 in 1939 to 65 in 1941, and only 46 in 1942. Even the number of foreign films shown in Britain dropped. Some of the features made, however, had a war setting, Noel Coward's *In Which We Serve* and Anthony Asquith's *The Way to the Stars* being particularly memorable examples. But more than 700 documentary films were made as this section of the industry blossomed. Unaided and, as the war developed, despite the Blitz and obsolete equipment, ACT members turned out official films,

OWING TO THE EXEMPTION OF CAMERAMEN FROM NATIONAL SERVICE, THERE HAS BEEN A TERRIFIC RUSH ON THE LOCAL CAMERA SHOPS

BUT YOU CAN'T TAKE ME SERGEANT—LOOK!

SO CLAUDE, OUR CLAPPER BOY IS TRYING THIS

Grouse-shootin' and ACT

The 1944 agreement with the Newsreel Association had an interesting prelude in the form of an incident involving Alf Tunwell, a cameraman, and British Movietonews. In 1943 Alf Tunwell had been employed by British Movietone as a first-class cameraman for 14 years, but he was asked that year to go out on a hazardous assignment in the western Mediterranean, based on a Royal Navy battleship. Alf was quite prepared to do the job - 'recording by cinematography battle scenes and other incidents of war' - but he was unhappy about the insurance provisions that had been made. Instead of being insured for £5,000 like the officers, British Movietone were only insuring him for £2,000 and he felt that if he died, that was a paltry sum to leave his widow, especially since informally, at any rate, a cameraman's job was reckoned to be the same rank as captain upwards. But when Alf refused to go unless he was insured for the higher sum, British Movietone sacked him. Compulsory arbitration procedures were in force during the war, however, so the case was taken to arbitration.

Sir Charles Doughty was the independent arbitrator, a man, George Elvin recalls, who was famous for having dived off the high board at Monte Carlo swimming pool wearing his monocle and come up with it intact, and Sir Gordon Craig represented British Movietonews. Alf Tunwell, accompanied by George Elvin and Sidney Cole, was depressed when they entered the arbitration room, because Sir Charles and Sir Gordon immediately began to chat about the grouse shoot they'd both been on the previous week, in some mutual friend's country estate. But George counselled calm because he had reason to believe that Sir Charles's considerations on Alf's case would not necessarily reflect a ruling class solidarity. George was right, because Sir Charles, with all due cordiality, insisted to Sir Gordon that he pay the right amount of insurance, ie £5,000, to cover Alf's mission, and that Alf be fully reinstated. And so ended the opening shot in a campaign to get newsreelers' work recognised as potentially hazardous, and the first small victory with a newsreel employer. As a result of it, Alf's colleagues got their insurance raised too, and many of them joined ACT.

Margaret Mulvihill

War experience

William Pafford - 'Paff' to generations of film and television technicians - draws on his memories of the Ally Pally transmitter of the war-time years.

'Since the official opening in 1936, television history has been well recorded, but there is one significant gap in the official version which needs filling in, namely the secret war-time activities at Alexandra Palace during the so-called 'shut-down' period of 1939-45. Although government policy was to stop all television transmissions at the outbreak of war, for obvious reasons, this policy was soon changed when the bombing raids started in London. By that time, it was impossible to recall civilian staff to maintain the transmitters for use against enemy radar. At the start of these operations against the nightly air raids on London, I was left in charge of a small band of dedicated RAF technicians brought in from the services for special duties at Alexandra Palace. There we worked (and slept) for the duration. Normally, we were on a 24-hour standby call.'

Left Allied soldiers are evacuated from Dunkirk. Forced to retreat to the Channel coast by advancing German tank units, British, French and Belgian soldiers are evacuated by boat to England. **Inset** Arthur Graham (second left) among former members of the Army Film and Photo Unit at their annual reunion, March 1983.

propaganda films and entertainment films that were first-rate. It was a time, too, when women first began to join the union in significant numbers, and took on less anonymous roles in film production. (It should be pointed out, however, that ACT never condoned unequal pay for equal work, George Elvin having a strong personal commitment to the elimination of sex-based differentials in pay).

The war enabled ACT to prove a fundamental point, namely, that there was no need to continue to import large numbers of foreign film technicians in order to keep a healthy and vigorous film industry going. It should be said, however, that the union was never xenophobic in its attitude to technicians from abroad, realising that the employers often operated on a global scale, and that

Right and **Centre Right** Training army film unit cameramen at AFPU studios at Pinewood. **Below** Dunkirk.

they tended to play off one nation's technicians against another's. Refugee film-makers were welcomed during the war and the union did everything it could to facilitate either temporary membership or full membership for them.

ACT's war record was used to great effect in negotiating with employers during the 1940s. As a result of its contribution to victory and its 'respectability' the union got many important agreements signed, notably the first agreement with the Association of Specialised Film Producers and with the British Film Producers Association. Then, in 1944, came the first agreement with the Newsreel Association. It was when the Newsreel Association was resisting ACT's demand for proper insurance cover on the grounds that cameramen's work was not hazardous that the film *Cameramen at War* (made by World Wide Pictures) was shown to the arbitrator presiding over the dispute. This was the first time that a film had been submitted and accepted as evidence in an industrial dispute and the result was a 100 per cent award on that particular matter.

The war epoch of the union's history ended with another victory, this time for the lab workers whose thirteen-week-long dispute in 1945 ended with substantial

Bottom Right Memorial board at Pinewood.

pay rises and greatly improved working conditions. Incidentally, the union's hard-won 'respectability' was reflected in the amusing conclusion of an arbitration case, this time versus the BFPA, which arose on another occasion. ACT had claimed an increase in location allowances for members, ie a small sum to be paid to members working away from home, and in due course the arbitrator pronounced, "Mr Elvin, I have decided to make my answer in your favour and as your members are professional gentlemen I shall make it in guineas". So £5 became five guineas, a useful little award, much to the BFPA's chagrin!

Denham at war
George Rains remembers his war-time days in charge of the film vaults at Denham Studios.

'When World War Two broke out, things got quiet in the studios, though a number of good war films were made. But since the studio at Denham was remote from the laboratories, we didn't meet or mix as we had done at Elstree (where George Rains worked previously). The laboratory became a hive of industry. Not only did we have a host of propaganda films to process, but lots of companies sent their films to us as they were ordered to clear them out of London because of the fire risks due to the bombing. So, soon my vaults became chock-a-block and more had to be built. At weekends when there was no night staff working, we fire-watched all night on a rota basis and travelled home in the winter nights in trains with blacked-out windows, running at 12 miles an hour.'

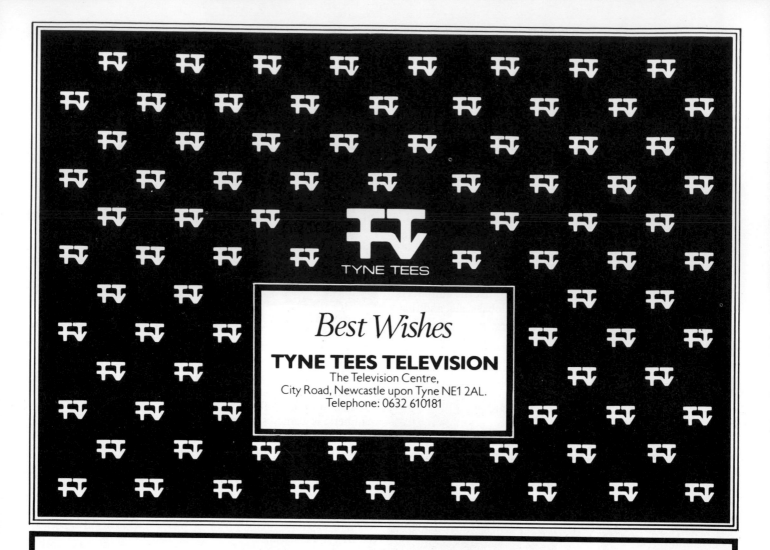

1945
PEACETIME BATTLES

Τhe war over, a golden age seemed about to
dawn. But there were clouds on the
horizon...

1945 brought in a Labour government on a
landslide victory, a government that, more than
previous governments, was interested in what
ACT as the representative organisation of
British film technicians had to say about the
future of the British film industry. It was not
overlooked, moreover, that the film industry
was a potential dollar-saving industry, both
negatively and positively, in that it could save
dollars in proportion to the number of
American films that were not being imported –
in the aftermath of war some 70 per cent of the
films being shown in Britain's cinemas were
American – and it could earn dollars to the
extent that British films were being distributed
in dollar-earning countries. In addition to these
vital considerations in the
impoverished post-war
financial
climate,
ACT
pointed out
that, unlike
many other
industries,
films
were
almost

Below The young Harold
Wilson (seated next to Ken
Gordon at an ACTT
conference) took a close
interest in the film industry
as President of the Board of
Trade in the Attlee
Government.

entirely a non-import consuming industry - raw materials such as steel or iron ore did not have to be brought into Britain in order to produce the final product. All that was needed was the raw stock (made in Britain) and, vitally, fair trading conditions. It was historically true that the system of distribution and exhibition of films in Britain was created as an apparatus for the distribution and exhibition of American films, with the result that the British producer had little or no bargaining power in relation to the distributor to ensure that his, or her, films were shown. From the Labour government, therefore, ACT wanted special assistance and encouragement for a film industry that was operating in competition with the American film industry, which, because of its size and its historic role in Britain, was able to dominate the native film industry effortlessly.

The need for diversion among the men and women in the Services and in the factories, and the huge number of foreign troops stationed in Britain, had swelled war-time cinema attendances. This pattern continued immediately after the war, and ACT members enjoyed a brief golden age of full employment. When the time came for the by now customary ten-year review of the Cinematograph Films Act, in 1948, Harold Wilson, the precocious President of the Board of Trade, and Jennie Lee MP, later to become Minister of Culture, took account of the wishes of the film unions. The National Film Finance Corporation emerged from this Act, a channel, the only one, through which a film production company without financial resources of its own, could get funds. Here, finally, was an institution, which, it was hoped, could as a matter of policy engage and give new opportunities for

British film-making talent.

But there were clouds on the horizon. By 1949, cinema audiences had declined drastically, and half of ACT's membership were jobless, while half of Britain's studio space lay idle and empty. The casualisation of the industry - endemic before 1933 and still haunting us to a great extent - set in. Though it aroused high hopes at the time of its foundation, the NFFC could not do much against the tide of crisis because it was still dependent upon distribution guarantees, or favourable reactions from distributors, before it would, or could, finance films - and, given the American-oriented distribution duopoly, it could not fulfil its brief as a means of encouraging a healthy and growing British film industry.

However, ACT took advantage of the NFFC's existence to set up ACT Films Ltd in 1950, the first film production company in the world to be owned and operated by a trade union. ACT Films saw the provision of work to many of its unemployed members as an immediate and urgent priority, but it was also a means of demonstrating that films of quality could be made to trade union standards of pay and conditions on moderate budgets. Unhappily, though, ACT Films were to be dogged by the problem that the NFFC could not and had not been designed to solve, namely the problem of getting distribution for British films. 1951 brought a new Conservative government and further crises. The closure of the Crown Film Unit (formerly the GPO Film Unit) in 1952, which had

Chance of a Lifetime -
In 1950 a 'good homely comedy' starring Kenneth More and Hattie Jacques came up against severe distribution problems, and even government disapproval, as a piece of 'dangerous Communist progaganda'. Directed by Bernard Miles, who wrote the script with Walter Greenwood of *Love on the Dole* fame, and shot by brilliant cameraman and veteran of British films,| Eric Cross, *The Chance of a Lifetime* became a cause celebre. The film's simple story line has a boss handing over his factory to the workers in a fit of pique after they've gone on strike over the sacking of a stroppy employee. The workers initially overcome the problems of management and look set for success when they market a new design of plough. But then they get into hot water, being unable to raise money from the bank and to deal with the intricacies of export marketing. Eventually, the workers realise they don't have all the skills that successful management requires, the old boss returns to save the day, and everybody at the factory accepts that they all need each other. But, in a show that was due to run and run, *The Chance of a Lifetime* was finished only to come up against a refusal from both the major exhibiting circuits on the grounds that its content was subversive. Then Harold Wilson, in his capacity as President of the Board of Trade, and the 1948 Cinematograph Films Act, came in to the story. Under the Act, the minister had the right to require a particular film to be shown on circuit, if an independent selection committee judged it suitable for exhibition as a British first feature by reason of its entertainment value. Accordingly, a selection committee was convened, and this committee pronounced that *The Chance of a Lifetime* was good entertainment. After Wilson had issued his direction, there was an entertaining scene when the representatives of Rank and ABC were called in to decide which of them would exhibit the film. They drew straws, and Rank drew the long one - thereby winning, or,in their terms, losing, the lot. But that was not the end of the incident, for Harold Wilson's directive was challenged in the cabinet, at a meeting presided over by Prime Minister Clement Attlee on 6 April 1950. According to the cabinet minutes, the then Minister of Labour (George Isaacs) said that, 'His advisers took the view that this film would be regarded as propaganda for Communism and for workers' control in industry, and it seemed doubtful whether it was expedient that the government should require an exhibitor to show it'. But Wilson won the day and the cabinet agreed that the Odeon Cinema Circuit should be required to show *The Chance of a Lifetime*, whereupon it proceeded to receive 'amazing notices' and did not, incidentally, precipitate a Communist revolution.

Peter Avis

ACTT
Congratulations on your 50th Anniversary

TV-am

Let's Celebrate

this year is the ACTT's **50**th Anniversary. And we've come of age **We're 21**

CTV
Channel Television
Serving the Channel Islands

Above George Elvin and Jennie Lee, MP, then Labour's Minister for the Arts.

specified that British television should be at least 80 per cent British in tone and content - a requirement that had been motivated by bitter experience of the Hollywood invasion in films - the union was suspicious of commercial television at first, believing, as did many Labour politicians, that standards of television would automatically decline if advertising were introduced. In fact, the momentous decision to organise in commercial television was carried at a General Council Meeting by only one vote.

But that decision was one of the most important that the union ever took. Luckily, the strength of the membership in features ensured that the television branch - responsible in 1956 for the addition of the second T - would be recognised. Even so, it was not plain sailing. It took a strike threat to ensure recognition in television in 1955 and many struggles before the first agreement was signed with the Programme Contractors' Association in 1957. That agreement symbolised the triumph of television and its permanent and prominent place within ACTT (at 7,000 plus members, the largest branch).

provided a substantial amount of employment for ACT members and had set standards of production that were the envy of the world, was another nail in the coffin. The free cinema passes made available to unemployed members, courtesy of Sidney Bernstein of Granada Theatres Ltd, so that they could keep in touch with 'current production activity', though appreciated, were hardly consoling as most of the films being shown in British cinemas were not home-produced.

In many ways, however, the union was better able to resist the decline. Following the bitter and unsuccessful Repair and Despatch Strike of 1946 the three main films unions - ACT, NATKE and the ETU - hammered out the historic Demarcation Agreement. As a result of a bit of 'horse-trading' - ACT gave up its projectionists to the ETU in exchange for sound technicians, while NATKE gave up scenic artists in exchange for distribution workers - long-standing differences were resolved, and, as the Film Industries Employees Council, the unions put up a united front against adversity. In January 1951, the enormous trade union demonstration that took place at Wyndham's Theatre in London, dramatically focused government and public attention on the plight of the British film industry and the determination of its workers to fight back.

But as one star, that of feature production, was falling, another star, that of television, was about to rise. Since the war the documentary and shorts sections of the industry had expanded due to the increasing non-theatrical use of films. As newsreel membership declined due to the virtual demise of two of the five newsreel companies, and feature members were unemployed, these sections were to come into their own with the advent of commercial television, approved by Parliament in 1953. Although it was largely, if not wholly, due to ACT that the Act inaugurating commercial television

It put TV technicians at the forefront, salaries and conditions-wise. The union knew, as did the employers who spoke of a 'licence to print money', that the health of the film industry as a whole and the long-term capacity of the features side to recover and re-establish viable British film production depended to a large extent on the resilience and strength of the television members. In 1958, when the union celebrated its 25th anniversary, it was still a young organisation working in a changing industry. But it was now mature, having come through an active childhood and a hard-working adolescence. From a handful of pioneers in 1933, it had built up a membership of nearly 8,000 into a strong and cohesive force.

Above Rehearsing *Cool for Cats* at Wembley Studios — A popular 'intimate' record programme from Associated Rediffusion.

A lot of our stars never reach the screen.

Thames Television has an unrivalled reputation for excellence in programme-making – a reputation reflected in the numerous international awards and the equally prized distinction of consistently high audience popularity. At the heart of this achievement lies the working relationship between Thames and its staff – including those stars behind the scenes, the members of ACTT.

Such acclaimed productions as Prix Italia winner 'Beauty, Bonnie, Daisy, Violet, Grace and Geoffrey Morton' and Emmy award winners 'The World at War' 'Edward and Mrs. Simpson' and 'Voyage Round My Father' would not have been possible without the technical expertise and professionalism of ACTT members. Their dedication and enterprise has helped maintain the high quality of programming associated with Thames Television.

Everyone at Thames wishes to congratulate the ACTT on fifty years of achievement and to acknowledge the part it has played in the development of television as we know it today. We look forward to many more years of continued success together, producing programmes synonymous with quality and excellence.

306-316 Euston Road, London NW1 3BB.

1955
NEW FRONTIERS

From the stormy advent of ITV to the burgeoning of the new media in the 1980s, the challenges to the union have never ceased.

In the quarter of a century since the union added the second 'T' to its name, many battles have been fought, the painstaking business of organisation and negotiation has gone on and the union has extended its activities to new areas of the fast proliferating communications industry.

Educational technology, independent local radio and latterly the burgeoning video industry have all come within the union's scope, complicating its tasks and enriching its mix. In March 1983, when the union gave itself a new structure − more democratically based and recognising the importance of regional organisation − it also updated the description of the areas in which it works. Instead of organising only in the 'film, television and allied industries', it now sees its function 'in the industries engaged in the production, processing,

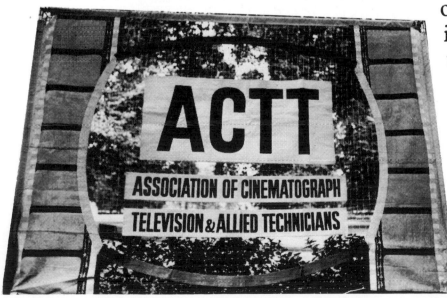

A DAY IN JULY   AFFAIRS OF THE HEART   A FINE ROMANCE   AFTERNOON OFF
AGONY   ALL YOU NEED IS LOVE   A MUSICAL PORTRAIT OF SIR MICHAEL
TIPPETT   AN AUDIENCE WITH DUDLEY MOORE   A PROFILE OF BENJAMIN
BRITTEN   AT THE HAUNTED END OF THE DAY   AQUARIUS   A QUESTION OF
SEX   BILLY LIAR   BLADE ON THE FEATHER   BLESS ME FATHER   BOUQUET
OF BARBED WIRE   BRIAN MOORE MEETS CAPTAIN MARK PHILLIPS   BRUCE
FORSYTH'S BIG NIGHT   BUDGIE   CANDID CAMERA   CANNON AND BALL
CATWEAZLE   CHAS & DAVE   CLIVE JAMES ON TELEVISION   CREAM IN MY
COFFEE   CREDO   CROWN MATRIMONIAL   DAVID FROST   DERBY DAY
DIAMOND   CRACK   DIAMOND   DICK   TURPIN   DISCOVERING   LONDON
DOCTOR IN THE HOUSE   DOCTORS AND NURSES   EIGHTEEN MONTHS TO
BALCOMBE STREET   EMU'S CHRISTMAS ADVENTURE   END OF PART ONE
ENEMY AT THE DOOR   FACING DEATH   FREDDIE STARR   GAME FOR A
LAUGH   GLOO JOO   HARK AT BARKER   HELEN – A WOMAN OF TODAY
HOLDING ON   HOLDING THE FORT   HOW TO STAY ALIVE   IF THERE
WEREN'T ANY BLACKS YOU'D HAVE TO INVENT THEM   INTIMATE STRANGERS
IT'LL BE ALRIGHT ON THE NIGHT   IT'S ALL IN THE GAME IN'T IT?   JASPER
CARROTT   JUST WILLIAM   KIDS   KINVIG   **ALL THE BEST FOR THE
WEEKEND FROM LONDON WEEKEND TELEVISION**   LILLIE   LIVE FROM HER
MAJESTY'S   LONDON TALKING   LOOK HERE   LOVE FOR LYDIA   LOVELY
COUPLE   LUCKY FELLER   MACMILLAN'S MAYERLING   MAGGIE AND HER
MANHUNT   METAL MICKEY   MIND YOUR LANGUAGE   MIXED BLESSINGS
MOONLIGHT ON THE HIGHWAY   MUHAMMAD ALI'S GREATEST HITS
NICKLEBY AND CO   NIGHT OF A HUNDRED STARS   NO HONESTLY   NO
THAT'S ME OVER HERE   OLD TIMES   ONE FINE DAY   ON REFLECTION   ON THE
BUSES   OUR SHOW   OUTSIDE EDGE   PAM AYRES   PEOPLE LIKE US   PETER
COOK AND CO.   PIG IN THE MIDDLE   PLAY YOUR CARDS RIGHT   PLEASE SIR
POLICE FIVE   PUNCHLINES   RAIN ON THE ROOF   ROMANY JONES
ROWAN ATKINSON PRESENTS   RUSS ABBOT'S MADHOUSE   RUSSELL
HARTY   SAMMY AND BRUCE   SATURDAY ACTION   SATURDAY NIGHT PEOPLE
SEARCH FOR A STAR   SEVEN AGES   SEVEN FACES OF WOMAN   SKIN
SOLDIERS   SPEAK FOR YOURSELF   SPORTS WORLD   STALIN   STANLEY
BAXTER   STARTING OUT   SUPERSONIC   SWEENEY TODD – THE MAKING OF
A MUSICAL   THE ADVENTURES OF BLACK BEAUTY   THE AWEFUL MR
GOODALL   THE BIG MATCH   THE DANNY LA RUE SHOW   THE DEATH OF
ADOLF HITLER   THE DO-GOODERS   THE FAITH BROWN AWARDS   THE
FENN STREET GANG   THE FOSTERS   THE GENTLE TOUCH   THE GOLD
ROBBERS   THE GOODIES   THE JAY INTERVIEWS   THE KRANKIES   THE LARRY
GRAYSON HOUR OF STARS   THE LAST NIGHT OF THE POMS   THE LAW
MACHINE   THE LONDON PROGRAMME   THE LONDON WEEKEND SHOW
THE MANY WIVES OF PATRICK   THE OLD CROWD   THE PINK MEDICINE SHOW
THE PROFESSIONALS   THE PYRAMID GAME   THE RAG TRADE   THE
SALESMAN   THE SEVEN DIALS MYSTERY   THE SHATTERED DREAM   THE SIX
O'CLOCK SHOW   THE SOUTH BANK SHOW   THE TOMMY STEELE HOUR   THE
TOP SECRET LIFE OF EDGAR BRIGGS   THICK AS THIEVES   THOMAS AND SARAH
TOMMY COOPER   TWENTIETH CENTURY BOX   TWO PEOPLE   TWO'S
COMPANY   UPSTAIRS, DOWNSTAIRS   WEDDING DAY   WEEKEND
WORLD   WE'LL MEET AGAIN   WHO DO YOU DO?   WHOOPS APOCALYPSE
WHY DIDN'T THEY ASK EVANS?   WITHIN THESE WALLS   WORLD OF SPORT

London Weekend Television

reproduction, transmission and distribution of film, video and/or audio material, and allied industries'.

These busy years have witnessed further ebbs and flows in the fortunes of the British film industry, which has become

increasingly casualised and increasingly subject to the whims of American financiers. The sheer quality of British film technicians has brought work to the remaining studios - now mostly 'four-wall' - and their creations have been heaped with honour in the academies of the world.

Often against the tide, ACTT has persistently campaigned for the development of an indigenous British film industry, as an expression of British culture, backed up by the prestige and resources of a properly funded National Film Authority.

The going has often been hard. But, bolstered by the safeguards that are built

Below Front page of *Film and TV Technician*, the ACTT journal.

into ACTT's feature agreement - including the crucial provision for pre-production meetings that was introduced in the early 1970s - the union has done much to save those who work in the film industry from the jungle-like existence that was their lot in the 1930s.

The battle to save the studios was dramatic, and attended with both success and failure. Shepperton and EMI Elstree were saved. But the MGM studios at Pinewood were lost - thanks to the boardroom vandals of Kellogg cornflakes in the US who took over that roaring lion

Above Union members and officials visit MGM after its closure.

of the screen and promptly chopped off its British arm.

Then there were the legal battles, which the union had reluctantly to engage in if it was to maintain its industrial strength within the film industry. The most significant courtroom tussle was between ACTT and the Boulting Brothers in 1964, after which it was established that a producer who was not in an entrepreneurial capacity had indeed to be a union member.

In recent decades, those working in the film laboratories have taken a heavy buffeting from the extension of new technology and from the insidious practice of the multinationals in switching production across frontiers to maximise profits. The diminishment of Technicolor from 1,200 to 300 employees is the most striking example of this evolution. Latterly, the importation of used prints from the US - against which ACTT has vigorously campaigned - has wreaked havoc with British laboratory workers' jobs, while at the same time subjecting British film-goers to an inferior product at the cinema.

And yet the laboratories remain the industrial powerhouse of the union. Time and again, while always being ready to defend their own interests, the lab workers - with their largest battalion at Rank Denham - have come to the aid of other sections of the union's membership when the call has been made.

It is fitting that a union whose early members were among the most creative documentary film-makers of the 1930s

The evolution of FTT

'A new journal is born. We make no apologies and offer few explanations.' Such were the first words written by the Editor (who was at one and the same time the union's General Secretary) in volume 1, number 1 of the *Journal of the Association of Cine Technicians* in May 1935.

Offering nevertheless a 'few explanations', the Editor went on to say that the new publication which cost 9d 'will offer a link between film technicians, provide an outlet for their views, help them in their work and through them benefit the film industry generally. Views expressed will be both critical and constructive, each contributor will be specially qualified in his particular line and whether we agree or not with his point of view there should be much to learn. The first list of contributors represents men whose opinions will be valued and whose remarks will be noted. Let us learn from them and so help the industry'.

Men, indeed, those first contributors all were — and presumably the readers were all men too. The first issue included a report on 'The Newsreel War', Alfred Hitchcock advising the young to 'acquire a real knowledge of cinema technique', Sidney Cole writing about 'Convention in Films', Otto Kanturek observing that 'sound films have robbed the cameraman of some of his thunder' and S S A Watkins pleading with directors 'to extend to their sound camera the consideration they gave to their picture cameras'.

In 1937, the title of the Journal was slimmed down to *The Cine-Technician* which it remained until it was renamed *Film and TV Technician* in January 1957. In the early years, the journal was brought out by various committee members. The first professional journalist to take on the task was Harold Myers, who was Editor from 1946 to 1948 and later went on to become a roving international correspondent for *Variety*. The annual report of 1947 said what a fine job Harold was doing by getting the publication out on time and doubling the circulation.

Beginning as a quarterly magazine, the Journal became bi-monthly in 1937 and monthly in the 1950s. Since 1964, it has been distributed free to all members and in 1974 it took on the present paper format. In 1982 *FTT* was judged to be Britain's best 'Trade Union Newspaper' in the TUC annual competition.

Peter Avis

Journal editors

Harold Myers 1946-48
George Mason 1948-50
Reg Groves 1950-55
Martin Chisholm 1955-66
Roy Lockett 1966-79
Nigel Wilmott 1979-80
Peter Avis 1981

Before 1946, the Journal was edited by various groups of committee members.

Left 1935 cover of the first issue of the union journal. **Above** The award won by *FTT* in 1982.

When a future government recognises the need to return to the traditions established by the Crown Film Unit and the COI, ACTT technicians will be ready to fulfil again their creative role in whatever new structure is introduced.

The new frontiers of television have been pushed back dramatically since 1955. ACTT has had the duty of protecting and improving the conditions of the technicians working in ITV and of picking up the pieces when - in 1968 and 1981 - franchise reallocations have been made with cavalier regard for either those who work in the medium or those who watch it.

The challenge of new technology has provided technicians with opportunities to enhance their skills and faced them with the problem of securing their continued employment. One of the main achievements of the resilient Television Branch and its National Organiser Jack O'Connor has been to win agreements whereby new technology - notably the ENG (electronic news gathering) camera - is introduced with a guarantee of no redundancies and with wider areas of the workforce being trained in the new techniques. Progress has to be for people as well as for machines.

Beyond television as we know it - and ACTT has had a presence in the medium ever since the BBC sent out those first signals from Alexandra Palace in 1936 - there loom the challenges and dangers of cable and satellite in the 1980s and 1990s.

At its Annual Conference in March 1983, the union laid down its own guidelines for this development. ACTT has no intention of being a break upon the future; it recognises, in the terms of its conference resolution, 'the benefits for feature and television film production and the plurality of choice for viewers offered by the controlled introduction of new methods of dissemination'.

But the union requires the introduction of a widely representative body to regulate the growth and operation of cable television. It is not willing to see Britain

should have been at the heart of the struggles to save a publicly-owned film unit of the post-war years. In 1973, ACTT was successful in preserving the Central Office of Information film unit from closure by its demonstration that the public purse would lose rather than gain from privatisation. In 1982, in the face of a government more resolute in its determination to break up public enterprise, the union was able to obtain enhanced compensatory arrangements for those whose permanent employment was ended, but it was not able to protect the prestigious film-making unit from the government axe.

Right Thames TV ENG crew at work.

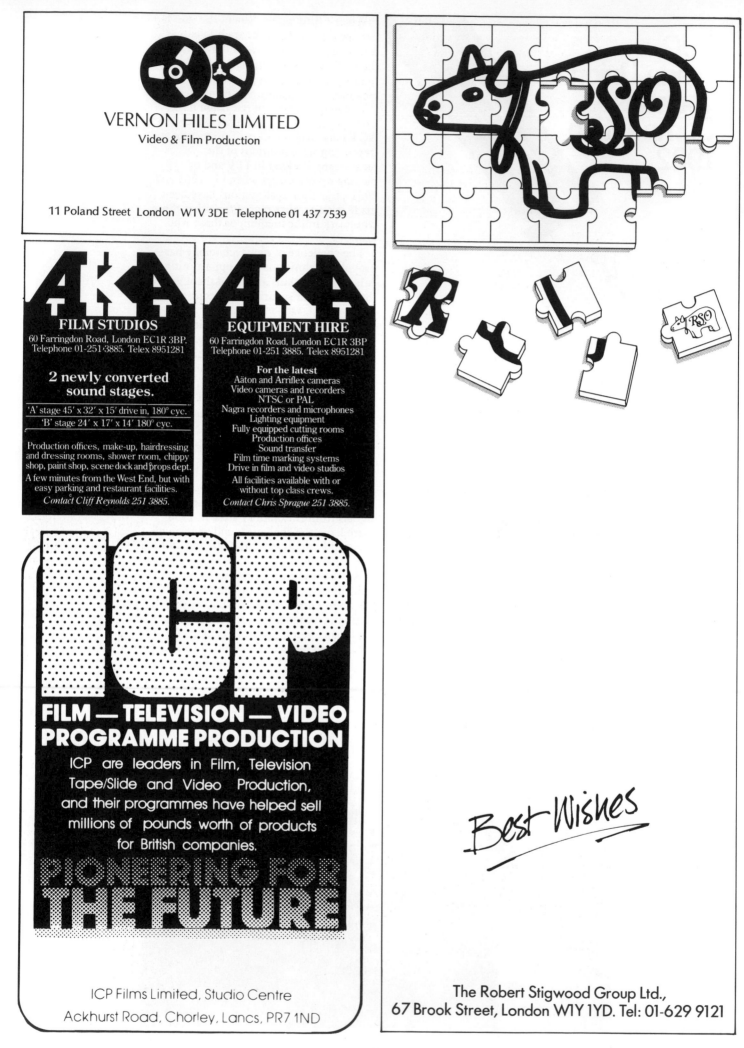
36

flooded with foreign products, to the detriment of its own industry and to the damage of its national culture. ACTT demands a democratic and publicly accountable system of franchise allocation and a statutory separation of interests between ownership, programming and supply.

ACTT - which provided the major stimulus to the establishment of the National Film School - has been in the forefront of those working to create industry-wide training schemes in film and broadcasting. Until such schemes are general, many people working in the industry will be condemned - by their lack of instruction or their sex - to ghetto areas in which ambition is thwarted and talent withers.

The union has always been outward-looking, with a sharp sense of the need to make the media serve the community rather than the profit-makers. It was Ralph Bond, then a Vice-President, who proposed the historic Resolution 42 at the 1962 TUC, where the unions first committed themselves to advancing the arts. From that resolution came the brief flowering of Centre 42, brainchild of playwright Arnold Wesker. Too little has

been achieved in this direction since, but the awareness that workers do not live by bread alone and that unions do not exist only to fight on the immediate issues of pay and conditions is expressed in the expanding workshop sector which ACTT has championed in the 1980s.

There is a growing realisation that the media are not neutral, and that those who own and control the media are prone to put over the message that serves them - and their allies - the best. Bias in the media, now the subject of widespread political debate and intense academic study, was brought to the notice of the trade union movement through the efforts notably of ACTT and the National Union of Journalists.

In the 1980s, ACTT has moved a long way from that little group of studio technicians who came together to defend their common interest in 1933. That same motive of common interest nearly brought about an amalgamation with the Association of Broadcasting Staff in 1979. It will undoubtedly eventually lead to the creation of a common union for the entertainment industry, set as a goal by ACTT's Annual Conference of 1981. But the spirit of 1933 need never be lost.

Right The 1981 Peoples March for Jobs was recorded by ACT Films.

Congratulations to the ACTT on their 50th birthday, from KAY, who've been servicing the industry since 1911.

CELLULOID FRONT

When the film laboratory workers began to join ACT in 1935 they added to the union's industrial muscle. And it is muscle they have often used to protect their own — and other members' — working conditions.

Membership had just topped the 750 mark when laboratory workers began to join ACT, and George Elvin, Ken Gordon and Sid Cole had a lot to do with the early recruitment. In one way or another, they managed to meet lab workers and gain their interest in a union. This concentration on lab recruitment went on from August to December 1935, and during that period the first 80 members were recruited who were to form the hard core of a branch of the union that contained 3,000 members by 1958. Charles Parkhouse, Sid Bailey and Cyril Philips, who became the first Chairman of the Laboratory Section, were three of the first lab members, who were soon operating on a branch basis.

Left Ken Gordon, who helped to recruit in the labs, takes time off on the dance floor. **Below** The Vinten Rotary picture and soundtrack printer.

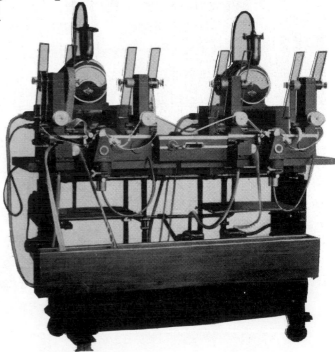

At that time there were about 15 laboratories, all paying just what they liked to their staff, with working conditions fluctuating wildly and no employers' organisation through which a common policy could be discussed. Eventually, however, the Film Production Employers' Federation emerged, and the lab workers were able to present it with their demands. But they had no intention of responding to them, and only gave in after the labs staged a complete stoppage at the time of George VI's Coronation. Then, they gave in to the idea of negotiating, rather than the demands, and the first agreement emerged only in 1939.

Above The first Lab. Agreement is signed, February 1939.

This agreement was a landmark. Guaranteeing two weeks' holiday with pay, sickness payments as well as improved wages and everyday working conditions, it covered 14 film processing laboratories and was the first agreement negotiated by ACT with any employers' federation. In due course, the laboratory section sought to terminate this agreement and negotiate a better one, but in the meantime the employers' organisation had disbanded. Although the first agreement was still binding - thanks to the crucial fair wages clause in the 1938 Cinematograph Films Act - there was no authoritative body with whom improvements could be negotiated.

Owing to the war, the lab workers were in need of a cost-of-living bonus - something that studio members had already achieved - and so the employers were taken to arbitration in order to get one. This move brought them together, of course, so in addition to receiving the bonus as a result of the arbitration proceedings, the lab workers also got a new employers' federation.

When an agreement had been hammered out with this new federation, however, the main body of the employers refused to endorse the work of their negotiating committee. ACT offered to refer the offending items, which related to wages and overtime rates, to arbitration, but at the same time threatened an official overtime ban in the industry if they refused to arbitrate. The employers refused to budge and so the ban came into operation in May 1945. Eventually, the dispute was referred to the National Arbitration Tribunal, which awarded completely in favour of the union. The arbitration award provided for:

☐ A 44-hour week in newsreel labs.

☐ Overtime payment for all hours worked before 8am and after 7 pm.

☐ Time and a half for nightwork.

☐ Equal pay for equal work.

☐ Rates for 17 new grades.

☐ Wage increases.

Now laboratory workers had, for the first time, decent wage packets and decent working conditions, and they had achieved it by sticking together in complete solidarity during a protracted and often bitter dispute. This victory was followed by some years of peaceful negotiation, but by 1953 the rising cost of living had eaten into the lab workers' hard-won agreements, and so once again, ACT approached the employers

Left (Early lab stalwarts — (from left to right) Stan Warbey, Len Runkel, Sid Bremson and Frank Fuller.

A show that ran and ran - the Kodak story

In the early war years Dufay Chromex at Elstree and Kodak Motion Pictures Division at Harrow were identified as important recruitment targets by the union's General Council. (Ilford Ltd was excluded because of the presence there of the General and Municipal Workers' Union). A number of workers at Dufay and Kodak had already indicated interest in union membership, and the recruitment drive at both plants took on a familiar pattern, involving the distribution of leaflets, the arrangement of meetings and a few lively campaigns. Ultimately, in May 1948, ACT signed its first agreement with Dufay Chromex, which was based on the first Laboratory Agreement of 1939 and this eventually applied to the Thames Ditton branch of the company, as well as Elstree.

But the struggle at Kodak was more protracted. In November 1949 a special ACT Kodak branch had been set up - previously Kodak members had functioned on a departmental basis - and its officers were Ken Roberts (Chairman), Dick Payne (Vice-Chairman), Ron Collins (Secretary) and Fred Morgan (Treasurer). This committee spearheaded the drive to organise the giant plant, which employed more than 5,000 workers. From the outset, however, the company resisted all trade union inroads, preferring as it did to operate in a paternalist way with the workers being accorded some privileges but no rights. They claimed that their existing workers' production committee, which had been established during the war years, was an adequate vehicle for employer/employee relations, and they did not stop at victimisation and intimidation of known union members in order to drive their point home.

In the end, it was not until December 1973 - 30 years after the first attempts at organisation there - that Kodak finally signed a limited recognition agreement with ACTT. This victory had an immediate history in the form of a struggle that began when Kodak members commenced a very effective work-to-rule in July of the same year, in an attempt to achieve basic shop floor rights. This action led to a direct confrontation with management and the company-sponsored house union, which resulted in a complete plant closure that lasted until the agreement was reached.

During that - hopefully the last - Kodak dispute, support for the members' cause came in a variety of ways, sometimes in the form of direct support and sometimes in the form of finance. The TUC gave official backing; the print union SOGAT fully co-operated by imposing restrictions on Kodak materials; TV Branch newsreel members switched their consumption to alternative film stocks; the T & GWU Dockers' and Drivers' Section, in conjunction with ACTT pickets, imposed severe blackings on Kodak goods and supplies. In addition, many SOGAT and NGA members introduced blackings and overtime bans, which, among other things, resulted in Kodak's house journal not being printed. Most heartening, however, was the international response to the well-known hostility of a multinational company to all trade unions - messages of solidarity poured in from Australia, Canada, France and Germany. It is with pride that we can record that ACTT was the first TUC-affiliated union to achieve recognition at Kodak, a recognition that was won at great personal and financial cost, but which bears out the truth of a traditional maxim of the labour movement - united we stand, divided we fall.

Margaret Mulvihill

42

Spies who never were

In March 1965 Ken Roberts and Geoff Conway were acquitted by the unanimous verdict of a jury of charges of industrial espionage. They were both long-serving Kodak workers and the charges brought against them reflected their employer's suspicion of trade unionists who had friendly relations with laboratory workers in other countries. In the course of the Old Bailey trial it was alleged that Kodak company secrets had been smuggled into the German Democratic Republic by Ken and Geoff in doctored tubes of toothpaste, and it was revealed that Kodak had paid £5,000 to the main prosecution witness.

Before this historic case was heard both the defendants, whose brief imprisonment provoked strong protest, were summarily dismissed, with the loss of all pension rights, while yet another Kodak employee was sacked immediately after the trial, simply because he had attended it. None of the three was reinstated as a result of the jury's not guilty verdict.

But that was not the end of the story. In 1968 the *Financial Times* published an article referring to 'real international spying' and a case 'involving Kodak', stating that the two men involved (eg Ken and Geoff) had been 'convicted'. Accordingly, a libel action was brought against the *Financial Times*, the journalist who had written the article and the printers. In due course the gravity of the libel was admitted, the smears were fully retracted, apologies were offered and substantial payments were made to the by-then much maligned ACTT stalwarts at Kodak. Subsequently, Ken Roberts became ACTT's Labs Organiser, while Geoff Conway joined the union's records and employment office.

Margaret Mulvihill

What Anthony Asquith, then the union President, said

'A case has recently been concluded at the Old Bailey in which two of our members were acquitted on a charge of industrial espionage. I, like you, congratulate them both on their being found not guilty. Like you, I am particularly concerned at the background on which the charges were brought. It was stated in court that Kodak Limited paid £5,000 plus a promise of a bonus to the chief witness for the prosecution. He had to go into the box for a second time to admit he had perjured himself on his first appearance.

Immediately after the acquittal of our two members, the General Secretary demanded from the management their reinstatement. This has been refused. Further, three members who attended the court on the final day having previously notified their management they would be absent from work, were subsequently suspended and one, the Chairman of Kodak Branch, has now been dismissed.

I cannot condemn too strongly such practices. Kodak should be utterly ashamed of themselves and I hope that even at this late hour they will appreciate the error of their ways, but if not I must stress to Kodak that as many employers have found out in the past, you do not defeat trade unionism by sacking trade unionists. We shall and must eventually get recognition from Kodak and the victimisation of a number of our members will, I know, only serve to strengthen our determination not only for recognition but the reinstatement of all dismissed members.'

Above Right Geoff Conway and Ken Roberts outside the Law Courts.

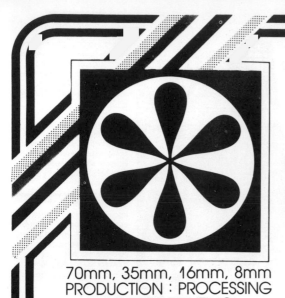

Above Alf Hunter of Technicolor presents the lab workers' case to shareholders' chauffeurs outside the Waldorf Hotel.

ACT shareholding - the bad fairy at Technicolor's annual shareholders' meeting

In 1951 the union decided to buy a small number of shares - as small a number as it was possible to get away with - in some of the major film companies, though only those whose shares were publicly dealt with on the stock exchange. Apart from the usefulness of receiving balance sheets for the purposes of negotiating, being a shareholder also brought with it the right to attend companies' annual shareholders' meetings. The union's policy on shares first paid real dividends during the lock-out strike at Technicolor laboratories in 1954. George Elvin, accompanied by some Technicolor employees and ACT members who had taken advantage of a company scheme to acquire a small number of shares, set off for the Technicolor shareholders' meeting at the Waldorf Hotel. Outside the hotel, ACT pickets distributed leaflets and inside the atmosphere was tense. The problem was that George was only a proxy shareholder because, in accordance with normal financial prudence, ACT's Technicolor shares were in the names of the union's trustees. As a proxy shareholder George was entitled to attend, but not entitled to speak. However, he was determined to speak, and did so. When the chairman proposed a dividend of 25 per cent, George got up and suggested that no dividends should be paid until Technicolor's staff were fairly paid and properly treated. The chairman reminded George that he was not allowed to speak, but George was surrounded by Technicolor members, so there was no way he could be forcibly ejected from the meeting. There was nothing for the chairman to do, but give in gracefully - in anticipation of what might happen, ACT had ensured that the Press were there in strength. The chairman suggested that he and George could meet soon and sort things out, which was just what ACT wanted, and a very successful settlement was negotiated.

Margaret Mulvihill

Alf Cooper

The inimitable Alf Cooper, like Bert Craik, has taken an active interest in all of the union's affairs throughout his long membership and is now an honorary member. He was a key 'insider' at Technicolor, where as a shop steward, and later a convenor, he was responsible for the recruitment of many ACT members. However, as a senior worker at Technicolor, Alf Cooper was not locked out in 1954 - instead he had to go on strike!

Bert Craik

Now an honorary member of the union, Bert Craik was appointed as ACT's organiser in 1942, having been an active member for seven years before taking on this job. It is typical of Bert Craik that he became a full-timer for the union at considerable personal sacrifice he left a far better-paid job as an optical printer at Denham Laboratories to do so. Although he has always taken a keen interest in the film industry as a whole, the lab members gained most from Bert Craik's dedication to their particular interest, and their story would have been a depressing one without him.

with a view to doing something about their deteriorating circumstances. But the employers refused to negotiate and pressed that the matter be referred to arbitration.

In 1954 a mass meeting of laboratory workers decided to impose an overtime ban and a work-to-rule. There followed a strike of 29 members in the developing department of Technicolor laboratories due to the management's threat to alter shifts during the period of working to rule. The management retaliated by locking out a further 800 members. A resolution from a mass meeting of 1,200 Technicolor members led to a meeting with the management, at which the company withdrew the lock-out notices and so this 'local' dispute ended.

But the employers as a whole were still refusing to negotiate. The working to rule continued, and was tightened up to the extent that all lab members broke for lunch together, and the principle of one person one job, and one person one machine, was strictly enforced. The employers responded with an ultimatum - announcing that unless the union withdrew the overtime ban and the instructions to work to rule, one week's notice would be given to all lab employees other than those required for care and maintenance work. When this lock-out took effect as

threatened, the whole machinery of the union was put in gear as part of a concerted effort to win the fight.

The maintenance engineers came out in sympathy with their locked-out fellow members and the complete stoppage lasted 12 days, as committees were set up at all labs and pickets were organised, including one outside the Waldorf Hotel during Technicolor's annual shareholders' meeting. In an effort to bring maximum pressure to bear on the union, the British Film Producers' Association gave support to the FLA and threatened to close down all film studios. At that stage the Ministry of Labour intervened and, after meetings with both sides, set up a committee of investigation into the dispute and requested that all forms of pressure be lifted - that is, the lock-out, strike, overtime ban and work-to-rule. Both the union and the lab employers were urged to agree to a resumption of work without victimisation. So the members returned to work and, as anticipated, negotiations commenced. In due course, a new agreement was reached, and a particularly gruelling chapter in the history of the laboratories closed. The Lab Branch of the union came out of the struggle victorious and with the confidence of a history in which complete and unfaltering solidarity had been maintained.

Wherever you set your sights,
you can depend on us!

The Travel Company and Renown Freight Ltd. have more experience moving the film industry than any other team in the UK. Our intimate knowledge of regulations and rates specific to film crews and their unusual freight assure our clients of the most comfortable and economical means of travel.

That's why people who depend on travel depend on us!

R ENOWN
FREIGHT LIMITED

the travel company

INTERNATIONAL LINKS

No one is an island — and no trade union should be either. ACTT has always had links — and often passionate concerns — across the world. In 1974, it was the main progenitor of FISTAV, the International Federation of Audio-visual Workers' Unions.

The cause of justice knows no frontiers. Throughout its history, the union has given its support to the harassed and the oppressed of many lands.

Before the Second World War, it helped refugees from the nazi regime in Germany. During the Cold War, it arranged work in Britain for the Hollywood film-makers hounded by the notorious Un-American Activities Committee.

ACTT has always opposed racism and has backed the Anti-Apartheid Movement from its inception. For years it joined campaigns against the Vietnam war and against the juntas that raped democracy in Greece and Chile.

In 1981, ACTT declared its support for the Solidarity trade union movement in Poland. It upholds trade union rights wherever and whenever they are threatened — and that includes Britain.

In supporting the Campaign for Nuclear Disarmament and other peace organisations, ACTT works for a world at peace in which the creative energies of trade unionists everywhere will enrich the lives of all.

Above Scene from *Spanish ABC*, made by Thorold Dickinson and other ACT volunteers who went to film in Spain during the Civil War, 1936-'39. **Centre** FISTAV conference. **Below** Fellow trade unionists demonstrate in South Africa.

FISTAV - the beginning

In 1974, 25 unions from 19 countries attended the founding conference in London of FISTAV, the International Federation of Audio-visual Workers' Unions. The organisation expanded rapidly, absorbing unions from every continent, from every area of communications and from nations with widely differing economic and political structures.

The origins of FISTAV can be traced to the three principal centres of film production in Western Europe - Britain, France and Italy. The film unions of these countries developed contracts over a period of 20 years before the idea of a wider association was born. The growth of co-production led these unions to develop bilateral relations with unions in Belgium, Finland, Ireland, the Soviet Union, Hungary and Poland. A first international meeting took place during the Cannes Film Festival of 1970, where representatives of workers in broadcasting were also present. Four years later, FISTAV was formally constituted, owing much to the initiative of George Elvin, at that time just retired as ACTT's President.

FISTAV is rooted in the recognition that only international trade union co-operation can challenge the growing power of transnational companies and regional economic groupings which would subordinate international communications to their own private interests. In the dawning satellite age, the exploding development of new technology impinges both on national cultures and on the employment, training, earnings and conditions of all those who work in the media. The response of workers in this environment needs increasingly to be a response organised across frontiers. FISTAV unions are capable of action in support of audio-visual workers in any country.

Peter Avis

FISTAV in action

In June 1976, Spanish film director Juan Bardem was arrested in Madrid. He had offended the Francoist authorities by organising a clandestine entertainment workers' union.

Alan Sapper, FISTAV President and Rene Jannelle, the Federation's Secretary General, appeared at a press conference in the Spanish capital, accompanied by several leaders of the banned union. The authorities, fearing international repercussions, allowed the press conference to go ahead. Juan Bardem was freed and renewed the struggle for the legalisation of the Spanish unions and liberation of all imprisoned trade unionists.

Peter Avis

49

WORLD WIDE SERVICE

TO FILM PRODUCERS AND TELEVISION PROGRAMME MAKERS

SAMUELSON GROUP PLC

EUROPE and AUSTRALIA

LONDON

SAMUELSON FILM SERVICE LONDON LIMITED

303/315 Cricklewood Broadway
London NW2 6PQ, England
Tel: 01-452 8090. Telex: 21430.
TeleFax: 01-450 3881
Cables: SAMCINE LONDON

LONDON

SAMCINE SALES LIMITED

303/315 Cricklewood Broadway
London NW2 6PQ, England
Tel: 01 450 4557, Telex: 21430
TeleFax: 01-450 3881
Cables: SAMCINE LONDON

LONDON

Samuelson Video

SAMUELSON VIDEO LIMITED
303/315 Cricklewood Broadway
London NW2 6PQ, England
Tel: 01-452 8090, Telex: 21430,
TeleFax: 01-450 3881
Cables: SAMCINE LONDON

LONDON

SAMCINE CASES LTD

100 Cricklewood Lane,
London NW2 2DS
Tel: 01-450 2141, 452 8090.
Telex: 21430,
TeleFax: 01-450 3881
Cables: SAMCINE LONDON

LONDON

SAMUELSON SIGHT + SOUND

303/315 Cricklewood Broadway
London NW2 6PQ, England
Tel: 01-452 8090, Telex: 21430,
TeleFax: 01-450 3881
Cables: SAMCINE LONDON

LONDON

SAMFREIGHT LIMITED

Rooms 41/43 G, Building 521,
London Heathrow Airport
Hounslow, Middx., England
Tel: 01 759 6011, Telex: 22197
TeleFax: 01-450 3881
Cables: SAMCINE LONDON

LONDON

Samuelson Lighting Limited

Dudden Hill Lane
London NW10 2DS, England
Tel: 01-452 5477, Telex: 21430
TeleFax: 01-450 3881
Cables: SAMCINE LONDON

AUSTRALIA

SAMUELSON FILM SERVICE AUSTRALIA (Pty) LIMITED

1 Giffnock Avenue
North Ryde 2113, nr. Sydney
N.S.W. Australia
Tel: 888 2766, Telex: 25188
TeleFax: 010 612 888 5691

25 Lothian Street, N. Melbourne
Victoria 3051, Australia
Tel: 329 5155, Telex: 35861

FRANCE

SAMUELSON ALGA·CINEMA SA

24/26 Rue Jean Moulin
94 Vincennes, Paris, France
Tel: 328 58 30, Telex: 670260F
TeleFax: 010 331 328 5077
Cables: SAMCINE PARIS

MAGIC BOXES

David Samuelson, who has known more cameras than most, looks at 50 years' evolution in cine equipment.

When our union was founded 50 years ago cinematography had just emerged from the chrysalis of the black-and-white silent screen into the types of images we know today. However, unlike the chronology of film production, it is difficult to tie particular technical developments down to individual years, or even an era, because technical development is a continuous process and even major advances take many years to become generally accepted. Still, some of the giant steps forward can be recorded in historic order and for our period the first of these was the coming of sound.

In 1928, just a few years before the union began, Baynham Honri had been on a mission to Hollywood on behalf of a leading British director, Alfred Hitchcock,

Below David Samuelson.

51

to investigate developments in sound on film recording and reproduction. He brought back and began to operate a recording system that was then introduced into the half-completed film, *Blackmail*.

If the coming of sound did nothing else, it established the electric motor as the sole means of driving both the camera and the cinema projectors in order to make the frames per second rate more constant than had been possible with hand cranking. Gone now was the regular use of 'creative' camera speeds, which, as the American film technology society (SMPE) noted, 'satisfied the public desire to have its picture drama projected under greater pressure with an increasing dose, bigger than life and one and a third times as fast'. Another effect of the coming of sound was that the cameras, after a brief period in sound-proof booths, were for many years to be swaddled in blimps to keep them quiet, an incarceration from which they did not emerge until comparatively recently.

In the early days the sound engineers ruled the roost. No matter where the images had to be photographed, the sound departments would attach their synchronous motors to the cameras and lay out heavy cables to their distant recorders, from where they would switch the cameras on and off remotely. When a

Right Jack Cardiff, director of photography, with Geoffrey Unsworth, operator, and a Technicolor camera. **Below** an early sound crew with Charlie Wheeler 'ruling the roost'.

film was shot on location a great heavy truck would lumber up into a predestined parking position; out would go a web of cables through windows, over roofs and down buttresses; a communication network would be set up; the microphone boom would be positioned in the pride of place on the set above the artists; and the

cameraman would be left to light around it as best he could. It was to be many years before technology completely gave way to the requirements of creativity.

The prestige of Technicolor

If the coming of sound was the big technical breakthrough of the 1920s then I suppose, on an international level, we must say that the really major advance of the 1930s was the development and introduction of the Technicolor three-strip system of colour photography and imbition system of colour print-making.

To be a Technicolor cameraman was to belong to an elite. Everything about making a film in 'Technicolor' was special, even the size and weight of the three-strip camera in its blimp, which required a block and tackle to put it on the tripod. These procedures were a far cry from the hand-holdable, silent-running, crystal-speed-controlled camera operations of today. One of my favourite Technicolor three-strip stories was told to me by Jack Cardiff, who once pointed to the row of six knobs on the back of the camera that had to be pulled out to release the rollers that held the film on the sprockets. He told me how, whenever he had a VIP visitor on the set, he would say to his focus puller, Denys Coop, or his operator, Geoff Unsworth, "Put in a bit more 'red'" and whoever was near the camera would twist one of the knobs, and so on. The visitors always left highly impressed, amazed at the wonders of modern technology.

The viewfinder revolution

The uneven application of technological breakthroughs is illustrated by the history of the mirror reflex shutter camera, the first of which was made in Britain in 1937 and in Germany in 1938. It was not until 1963, however, when Mitchell in the United States produced their first acceptable rotating-mirror camera, that

The Forth Bridge

As a charter member of ACTT, and a camera assistant in the early 1930's at the old BIP studios, Elstree, how well I remember the friendly visits of Brother George Elvin, who came down to tell us all of his plans for a union, and to canvas the members.

Being of rather conservative stock - inherited no doubt from my father, then Vicar of Darlington - I frankly didn't take too easily to some of George's doctrines. Late on Saturday afternoon, however, after working without extra pay on someone's wretched 'retakes', and spending my only reward - a one-and-sixpenny food voucher - on half a meal in the studio canteen; a big decision was made. I was 'converted' to George, as my father would have put it, and would now hope for better days. Thanks to ACTT, better days were not long in following.

While thinking BIP, my thoughts go back to two awe-inspiring pieces of early equipment, but I hold nothing against the studio, for we were all learning in those days. One was the camera crane, for which usually two days' notice was required before it was brought onto the set. The normal grip crew was far from adequate to handle this archaic piece of equipment, so on the day of the shoot, additional crews from neighbouring stages had to be brought in, much to the anguish of other directors whose productions were then held-up for a couple of hours. (The 'Press Gangs' were at work!).

The crane not only had to be pushed; it had to be pulled also; and part of the crew who 'rode' the crane were delegated to the 'raising' of it - a terrifying and precarious move for the cameraman, who could easily be catapulted to the roof. The anticlimax occurred when, after all this work and effort, the camera was raised to its maximum height, 14 feet from the ground, and the director moved in to inspect the shot from a small step ladder.

Another unforgettable piece of equipment was 'The Forth Bridge' - so named by the late director, Arthur Woods, with whom I had the pleasure of working on many epics. 'The Forth Bridge', masterminded by the sound department, was a shining steel mike boom of elaborate cantilever construction, which, by a scissor action on the part of the boom operator, could shoot the microphone across to any part of the set.

The gleaming scissor-like movement was a triumph for the sound department and a nightmare for the lighting cameraman. For no matter where he placed his source light, there would be multiple shadows and reflections all over the set. A cutter might stave off shadows from the 'top tier' of the 'Forth Bridge', but what about the 'bottom tier' which was often lower than the microphone itself.

Only once did I see a cameraman prevail over this monster. This was on a Hitchcock set where the characters were lit from the floor, to create a feeling of terror. Then we all smiled as we looked up to see the shadows of the 'Forth Bridge' dancing on the studio ceiling, well out of the shot!

Drummond Drury

this advance had a real impact. I think, for example, that *Tom Jones* (1962) was the first major feature film, certainly the first internationally successful one, to be shot on a mirror shutter camera.

Even before 1910, almost all professional motion picture cameras incorporated a facility that enabled the camera operator to view the image through the taking lens as it was focused on the emulsion layer in the camera gate. This image was used to check accurately the line-up of the picture area, to compare it with the image seen in the auxiliary viewfinder, which was subject to paralax errors as well as errors of coverage and displacement, and to check optical focus.

thing. None of these systems, however, could be used while the camera was running.

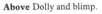

Above Dolly and blimp.

Experienced cameramen also used this image as an extinction-type exposure meter.

In the 1920s and 1930s a number of cameras were designed that incorporated a facility whereby the film in the gate could be replaced by a ground glass situated in exactly the same position in space. The best-known of these was the Mitchell NC, where the film transport mechanism, the film magazine and the camera drive could be displaced in toto to one side, bringing an optical viewfinder incorporating a ground glass screen in position behind the lens. At the same time, Slechter in Czechoslavakia and Eclair in France produced cameras where only the film in the camera aperture gate was retracted and replaced by a ground glass and a right angle prism, which lined up with an optical system on the outside of the camera. Newman & Sinclair in London produced a lightweight clockwork camera into which a right-angle prism, ground glass and an image magnifier could be inserted as a way of achieving the same

In 1937 Vinten introduced a camera that incorporated a revolutionary viewfinding system - a rotating mirror placed in front of the film plane at an angle of 45 degrees to an optical axis that acted both as a shutter to mask off the light while the film was advanced between exposures and reflected the light onto a ground-glass focusing screen to be viewed by the camera operator during this period. Although novel and innovative, this pioneering camera was not commercially successful.

Arriflex and Cameflex
In March 1938 Arnold & Richter, a Munich-based camera manufacturer, delivered to a cameraman in Berlin the 'first Arriflex hand-holdable camera (serial numbered 500). In addition to its rotating-mirror shutter reflex viewfinder system, this camera boasted many other innovations. It was light enough to be hand held; it used external 30 and 60-meter (200 and 400 foot) displacement magazines; the film pull-down movement

was a simple cam-operated claw movement combined with a pressure plate film gate that gave acceptable image steadiness at normal camera speeds; it had a DC electric motor drive (developed from a portable drill) placed underneath the camera that also formed a handgrip for support; and it had a rotating lens turret on to which a range of three lenses (28, 50 and 75mm) could be set without cutting in on each other. With remarkably few changes this basic camera design has continued in production for almost 50 years.

Arriflex reflex cameras were used extensively by German newsreel cameramen during the Second World War and became highly prized trophies when captured by Allied war correspondents. Stories are told of how, during the European campaign, a camera body with one magazine and lens would be captured, and a cameraman would go through fire in advance of the troops and risk his life to get to the German cameraman's base in quest of the spare magazines and additional lenses. After the war the Americans produced a camera which they called the Cameraflex, which was broadly similar to the Arriflex but had its drive motor set on the side of the camera instead of underneath it. It was not a successful product, however, and very few were made. In 1947 Eclair of Paris produced a reflex camera, which they called the 'Cameflex'. (It had to be called the Camerette in the United States to avoid confusion with the Cameraflex).

The Cameflex was also innovative for a number of reasons. It had a reflex shutter which incorporated a facility for exposure adjustment while the camera was stationary; a ratchet film pull-down movement that gave very steady pictures and a 200 degrees shutter opening (but which was none the less noisy and could not be run on reverse); an offset lens turret that permitted lenses of widely disparate focal lengths - from the widest

angles to the longest telephotos - to be mounted without cutting in on each other; an eyepiece that could be rotated to any angle; and a 'clip-on' magazine system with pre-formed loops that could even be attached and removed while the camera was still running. The Cameflex also had a very small and highly efficient interchangeable motor with a hand-turn and a clockwork drive as available accessories. In addition, it was good ergonomically, being almost the first camera (the German Askania was the first) which sat snugly on the operator's shoulder and made it possible to hand-hold lenses of long focal length with greater steadiness than ever before, and it had a companion lightweight metal tripod and pan and tilt head, which even incorporated a clamping system that allowed the head to be attached to items of furniture if need be.

Above Arriflex 35mm No 500, used in Berlin in 1938 and now in the Samuelson collection of veteran cameras. **Below** The golden Panaflex with panatape.

Sound on film and tape

The development of the Bach Auricon range of 16mm sound-on-film cameras in the 1940s represented another milestone in the history of cine equipment. Originally conceived as a simple amateur 100-foot loading, lightweight camera incorporating a galvanometer-type optical sound recording system and called the Cinevoice, this basic camera, albeit in a derivative form and much developed in many important details, went on to become the workhorse TV news camera in use all over the world even in the 1980s.

The most major development in sound recording technology since the development of sound itself was magnetic tape recording, which was in its turn a development from the magnetic wire recording system used by the Germans during the war. In the late 1940s a British sound recorder manufacturer, Leevers-Rich (headed by Norman Leevers), and an

American company, Rangetone, independently developed magnetic recording systems utilising sprocketless quarter-inch tape, whereby the audio sound would be recorded along one half of the tape and a series of one-volt ac electric impulses generated by a small ac alternator driven by a camera drive shaft that indicated the camera speed, recorded along the outer edge of the tape.

Later, by using this camera speed reference recording to control the speed of a sprocketed film recorder, it became possible to record sound on location without bulky or heavy equipment, and without the need for long cable runs between one unit and another. In consequence it became possible, especially when the Nagra recorder was introduced in the 1950s, to record sync/sound in any place where is was also possible to site a camera. This in turn was simplified even more in the 1960s with the introduction of precisely speed-controlled camera motors (using crystal control circuitry) and similarly frequency-controlled pulse generators that recorded the speed of the magnetic tape recorder at the actual time of recording.

Zoom lenses and anamorphs
The introduction of anti-reflective lens coatings in the 1940s made multi-element lenses a practicable proposition and this in turn brought forth the zoom lens. Zoom lenses were not entirely new, however, the first for cinematography having been designed by Cooke in Britain and manufactured by Bell & Howell in the United States in the early 1930s. But only a few were made, perhaps because cameramen did not appreciate what could be done with them. An American *Cinematograper Magazine* article of the period suggested that they be used for aerial photography to keep the magnification of the ground constant while the aircraft flew a level course over undulating terrain.

Below Cooke, Bell & Howell vary-focal length zoom lens invented in 1935. **Right** The original anamorphic lens made by Henri Cretien which became the first Cinemascope lens through which *The Robe* was photographed.

Perhaps another reason why these early zoom lenses never became popular was because focusing had to be done by

diopters and viewfinding by guesswork, a situation that was changed by the advent of the reflex viewfinder. By the late 1940s, a number of manufacturers had produced zoom lenses with limited focal length ranges, but it was from Som Berthoit (16mm type) and Angenieux (35mm), both of France, that really practicable zoom lenses with focal range lengths of 4 (later 10 and 20 and 1 by the 1950s and 1960s) came.

Another very important lens development of that period was the retrofocus or reverse telephoto lens, where the back focal distance clearance was considerably longer than the lens focal length. This enabled wide angle lenses to be used on reflex cameras. One of the first was the Angenieux 18.5, which could be used on an Arriflex 35mm camera where hitherto the shortest focal length that could be used was a 28mm.

Universal dimensions and standards
There are just three basic groups of standard that unite film-makers all over the world and make film unquestionably the most universal means of communication between all the peoples of all the continents. These are - the dimensions of the film and the position and sizes of the perforation of the film stock we use (35mm set by Edison in about 1889 and 16mm set by Kodak in

about 1924); the size, position and speed of the sound track (Warner Brothers about 1927) and the 2:1 anamorphic squeeze (20th Century Fox's Cinemascope in 1953). Everything else is embroidery.

Legend has it that in 1925 a famous French optical designer, Henri Cretien, saw Abel Gance's film *Napoleon* shot in the French Triptych system of three projectors set side-by-side to give a wide screen presentation (the French had a ten-projector full 360 degrees system called Cineorama as early as 1896). Cretien is reported to have said that he could achieve the same effect with a single camera and projector by using a system of anamorphic lenses that he had developed to give a wide angle view to tank drivers in the First World War.

Accordingly, test films were made in 1927 and shown in the United States in 1930 and then made again for the Paris

Exposition of 1937, but nothing came of any of them. It was not until 1953, when the security of the American film industry began to be seriously threatened by the spread of television, and before they had decided to join it rather than try to beat it, that they took another look at the wide screen, as well as 3-D, in an effort to make cinema-going a special experience. Yet again, Professor Henri Cretien travelled to the United States to demonstrate his Hyprogonar anamorphic lens system to the movie moguls of Hollywood. Among these were the two giants of 20th Century Fox, Spyros P Skouras and Darryl F Zanuck.

Zanuck's son Richard, once told me how the decision to resurrect the anamorphic process was taken. He recalled how his father and Spyros Skouras spent the whole weekend at Zanuck's country home in Palm Springs discussing the project. 'For hours they paced up and down before they came back into the house to say, "We're going to go with the French system, we're going to call it Cinemascope, and we're going to build wider sets for *The Robe* (which had already been shooting for six weeks) and start shooting all over again".'

With only a single anamorphic lens available, which had a chipped rear element and initially could be used only with a single prime lens, Fox embarked on one of the greatest gambles in the history of the film industry. When, later in 1953, *The Robe* opened to rapturous reviews and became an instant commercial success, the 2:1 anamorphic squeeze ratio had been irrevocably established and the shape of the big cinema screen changed forever. The farsightedness, vision and sense of showmanship of those two great entrepreneurs had been completely vindicated.

The state of the art

The past decade has seen an unprecedented proliferation of innovative developments in motion picture production equipment. There is hardly an item in general use by mainstream film-makers today, for example, that was in equally general use even before 1975 - less than ten years ago. The cameras, lenses, recorders and accessories we use, almost all of them have been much refined during the last decade.

In the field of 35mm cinematography it is now almost unthinkable to make a major motion picture without a camera that is as quiet as the studio in which it is used and hand-holdable when necessary. It will certainly incorporate mirror-shutter viewfinding; often it will have an optional facility for an auxillary television viewfinder; it will be battery-driven and have crystal control speeds at 24-25fps, as well as variable speeds; the camera speeds and footage shot will be read out by a digital display; the ground glass markings may be illuminated when shooting against a dark background; the shutter will often be adjustable, even when the camera is running; and film magazines accommodating various lengths of film can be fitted to it. Certain 16mm cameras commonly used for filming news events now have a through-the-lens exposure metering system.

Among the accessories available to the film-makers of today are 'floating camera' systems of hand-holding, which make it possible to move over undulating ground, or up and down stairs, without undue camera unsteadiness, while pan and tilt heads with 'fluid' bearings make it possible to start a camera movement without a sudden jerk, and remotely controlled camera crane hydraulic dollys that run on demountable tracks, facilitate completely controlled camera movements that can repeat up to 16 movements simultaneously over and over again to within an accuracy of 1/1,000 inch and so on.

All such developments are only important, however, if they contribute to better pictures on the screen and make the medium more attractive to the paying public. Instead of being simply dazzled, we must sometimes stop to ask ourselves, 'Would Shakespeare have been more readable if he had had a golfball typewriter and a word processor?'. It is the imaginative use of equipment technology over the years, not the equipment in itself, that has ensured the dynamism of the film industry over the past 50 years.

Below Camera crew on *Victor/Victoria*.

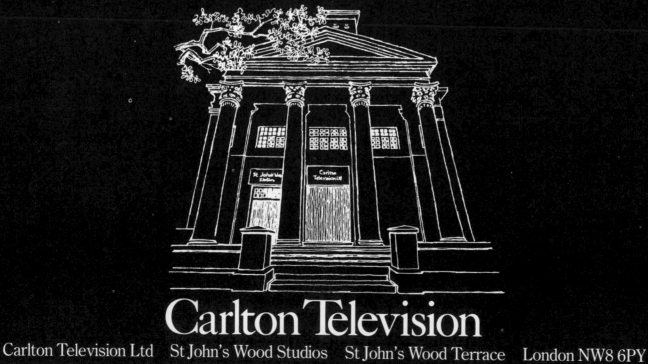

DOCUMENTING THE DOCS

The 1930s documentaries are now legendary. Ralph Bond wrote this personal testimony for the 'Cine-Technician' in 1955.

When I first joined ACT in 1935 the documentary school of film-making was almost exclusively confined to the GPO Film Unit, which itself was the successor of the Empire Marketing Board film unit created by John Grierson and Sir Stephen Tallents. I started off there as a general production assistant, and was promoted to the grand title of Studio Manager. However, it took me three months to induce the petty cash department to buy me a stool - not even a chair - to sit on (Grierson believed that everyone should be constantly on the move). Later, I was allowed to direct my first film, and in the years that followed I was to direct, produce and write films for a plethora of companies. But the experience with Grierson contributed two of the most exhilarating years of my life.

Right George Foster Noble, director of photography, *The Voice of Britain.*

I was not the first from the GPO Film Unit to join ACT - Roy Stocks had that distinction - but the two of us lured George Elvin down to Blackheath and before very long all the technicians became members. I was deputed to go to John Grierson and seek recognition. With some trepidation I expounded the purposes of trade unionism to him. He cut me short. "You don't have to tell me all that; I'm a member of the Transport and General Workers' Union." Talk about teaching your grandmother to suck eggs!

Above A still from *Night Mail,* directed by Harry Watt and Basil Wright, with a poetic narrative by W H Auden. **Below Right** Humphrey Jennings' *A Diary for Timothy* and **Left** Grierson's *Drifters.*

The studio at Blackheath was typical of those early rhapsodic days of documentary. It had been formerly a girls' school, and had been converted to our own requirements. At that time the GPO Film Unit had just completed its first feature production, *BBC Voice of Britain.* Stuart Legg, who many years later did such fine work for the Canadian Government Film Board, was the director under Grierson's producership, and I was the production manager. The material shot by Legg for this film, aided by Chick Fowle and Jonah Jones on camera, led to a

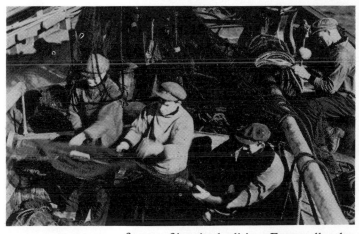

frenzy of inspired editing. Eventually, the entire unit was turned on to the job with Legg editing one sequence. Evelyn Spice (who also later went to Canada) on another, Basil Wright on a third, and other members of the unit mucking in as and when needed.

The unit expanded rapidly and the local pub at the bottom of the road where we all gathered at lunchtime became one of the show places of Blackheath. Benjamin Britten, William Coldstream, the painter, and W H Auden, the poet, had joined the regulars, while Cavalcanti, straight from his avant-garde successes in Paris, allied his own energies and enthusiasm to those of Grierson. Some wonderful films were made then in that little studio, which boasted only one carpenter and one electrician. Outstanding, of course, was *Night Mail,* directed by Harry Watt and Basil Wright, with a poetic narrative by Auden. Everything new in the way of ideas was avidly seized upon and chewed over by what Grierson chose to call 'the gang'. Experiment was the order of the day and if some failed, others succeeded brilliantly. Len Lye came in with the then fantastic theory of making a colour film by painting direct on to celluloid. He was given his head (and a tiny room) by Grierson, and the result was *Colourbox,* a film still relished by connoisseurs.

It was all too good to last. There was so much talent that the unit had to seek wider horizons or burst. Arthur Elton led the way by forming his own unit and making a documentary about the work of a labour exchange for the Ministry of

Labour. Edgar Anstey and John Taylor made *Housing Problems* for the Gas Company and this really caused a commotion. The film adopted the style of direct sound reporting of people living in the slums, and what they had to say was guaranteed to stir the heart of any citizen with a conscience. Then Anstey made *Enough to Eat,* a great social documentary on nutritional standards, with a commentary by Julian Huxley.

The spill-over from Blackheath to the cruel world of commercial as against public sponsorship continued. Donald Taylor had already formed his Strand Film Company, Paul Rotha did a series for GBI, and John Taylor and Basil Wright formed the Realist Film Unit. The

Realist Film Unit was notable for the high quality of its films, particularly in the educational and instructional fields, and for Frank Sainsbury, who expounded his theories of philosophical anarchism in every possible place and at every opportunity. No session at The Highlander (now the Nellie Dean) in Dean Street was ever complete without Sainsbury's presence, and no session with Sainsbury's presence ever ended without most of the assembled company losing their tempers.

By this time John Grierson had left the GPO and with Elton and Wright had formed Film Centre. When Grierson left Blackheath, he left behind him a flotilla of rear-admirals vying with each other for supreme command on the bridge. But the Realist Film Unit was the first documentary unit to sign a proper agreement with ACT. All honour to John Taylor for facilitating that first break, because other units then fell into line and eventually the rapidly growing number of documentary and short film companies formed themselves into the Association of Short Film Producers (subsequently renamed the Association of Specialised Film Producers). After strenuous negotiations, our first agreement with the ASFP was signed in 1943. It would be invidious to select the names of particular companies who contributed most to the growing national and international prestige of British documentary film-making - invidious, but to some extent unavoidable. I have already mentioned the Strand Film Company, Film Centre, GBI and the Realist Film Unit. Others that developed from this original grouping and maintained the high standard and integrity were (to mention just a few) - DATA (formed on co-operative principles), Basic Films, World Wide Pictures and the Shell Film Unit. One of the largest groupings of all the short and documentary makers was the Film Producers' Guild, with its associated studios at Merton Park. As the movement grew, and more sponsorship was attracted, more ambitious films were made, which required the kind of fully equipped studio facilities that were available at Merton Park.

It would be impossible to conclude these few notes without coming back to where I started - the GPO Film Unit. When the Second World War broke out, the GPO became the Crown Film Unit and moved to Pinewood, then later to its own studios at Beaconsfield. The personnel of the unit bore little resemblance to its early days, but the films produced during the war years made history, and I think it a lasting shame that in 1952 the government, for alleged reasons of economy, closed it down and deprived the country of its only publicly-owned film production unit.

A WOMAN'S PLACE

In the 1980s, ACTT has become committed to the policies of equality that many women have been advocating for decades. Sheila MacLeod talked to some of the women who have helped to shape the union's history.

Above Women at Greenham Common in 1983 make the point that arms are for linking.

Unlike their sisters in many other trade unions, ACTT women have never had to fight for equal pay because this principle has also been a practice throughout the union since its foundation. And yet the Annual Conference of 1981 voted by an overwhelming majority for the appointment of a full-time Equality Officer to protect the rights of women, as well as those of racial minorities, within the industry. An unnecessary move engendered by a caucus of feminist extremists? Or an indication that an organisation which has tended to be progressive in one area of women's rights will continue to be progressive in others? Well, as it happens, neither. The personal histories of women who have been active in the industry and/or the union reveal an altogether more complex (and rather more interesting) picture of female experience in the making of film and (later) television over the last half-century.

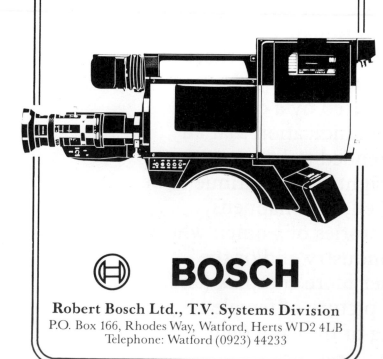
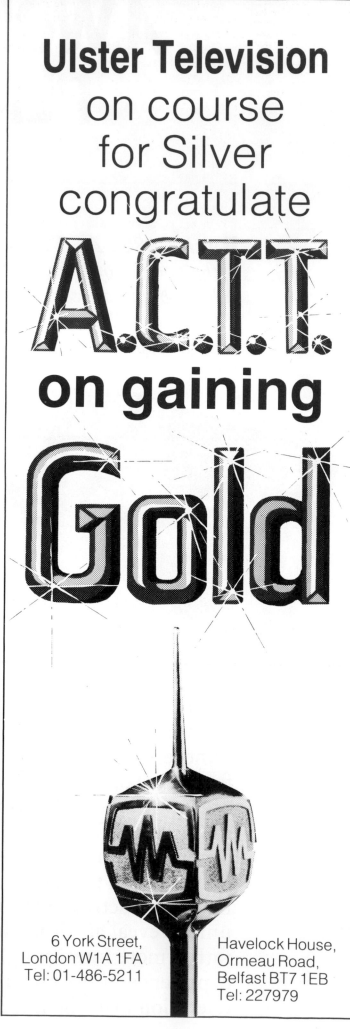

Right Women members played a big role in the 1981 campaign against the closure of Elstree TV studios and more than 30,000 signatures were gathered for the protest petition. Carrying some of the petition forms are Jill Rowland, film librarian, and Kirsten Hansen, promotions director — both staff at Elstree. **Below Right** Muriel Box (centre) with Barbara Murray and Peggy Cummins on location in Sloane Street for her film about women police, *Street Corner*.

The older women I spoke to were far more optimistic and sanguine than was the younger generation. There was a general feeling that this is a man's world (life, that is, rather than the film/television industry in particular) and that they were very lucky to have achieved what they had with such limitations. There was probably a certain amount of undue modesty inherent in this attitude - a matter of style quite as much as of content. Others had not had their opportunities, which was regrettable, but how could they protest about the way women were treated when they themselves had led such fulfilling lives, had had such wonderful times? To do so would be ungrateful, perhaps even hypocritical.

There is no doubt that there are exceptional women in each generation, and it was clear to me that all the women I spoke to were exceptional - as regards skill, talent, devotion, and, perhaps most important of all, stamina. But there is no doubt too that there are also exceptional times in which the prevailing consciousness is altered and, in shifting, reveals possible new patterns of existence complete with hitherto unrecognised opportunities. If this shift was brought about, for the younger generation, by the impact of the women's movement, for the older one it was caused directly by the effect of the Second World War and its aftermath on the film industry. This is not the whole story, of course - technological changes have also played a major part - but a consideration of these two important shifts helps to place individual testimonies in context.

Kay Mander

Kay Mander was the first woman to join ACT, having been recruited in 1935. Until 1940 she worked in continuity, but in the war years, 'when there weren't any men around, so it was much easier to get work', she wrote, edited and directed for the Shell Film Unit and later for Paul Rotha Productions. Her experience at Shell included tunnelling through debris in search of bomb victims. After the war she formed Basic Films with her husband, R K (Rod) Neilson Baxter, and a cameraman colleague. They made various films for government and industry, including a French teaching film, *La Famille Martin*, which won the British Film Academy Specialised Award in 1949. For most of the 1950s she lived in Java, where she and her husband set up a documentary/educational film department for the Indonesian government under the auspices of UN Technical Assistance. Here they trained local technicians and shot material for the Indonesian government, Shell, and the Children's Film Foundation. It was also for the CFF, back in England, that Kay Mander co-scripted and directed *The Kid From Canada*, which won a special award as a contribution to international understanding at the Venice Film Festival in 1956.

'From 1957 onwards I failed to get any satisfactory work as a director, so I went back to feature continuity, which I've been doing ever since. Michael Balcon told me quite flatly that women couldn't handle film crews and, anyway, there weren't any suitable films for women to direct.' Kay Mander tells the story of Balcon's rebuff with an incredulity tempered by amusement, but at the same time she refuses to see her return to continuity as a defeat. 'Of course directing is fun, because what you produce in the end is something you thought of yourself. But I don't really want to direct. As long as I'm working in films, I'm happy. That's the point - not being some sort of star. I enjoy working with actors, and I'd rather have a less prestigious job with good actors than work with bad actors where you have to compromise all the time. The great thing is to be working with professionals - by which I mean people with plenty of self-discipline.'

Professionalism may be largely a matter of self-discipline, but it is also a matter of training and experience - two commodities that are hard to come by in the film industry, perhaps especially for women. In the late 1940s Kay Mander was chairman of an ACT committee that aimed to set up apprentice and training schemes, but then, as now, it was a difficult aim to achieve. 'The idea of film school is all right as far as it goes. What they do is turn out directors. They do teach some techniques, but they don't teach how the various skills interlock and work together. The way to learn how to make films is by making films.' But, she insists, the difficulty of finding training is a problem for men and women alike.

to admit it was very good for women.' At the Realist Film Unit she was only one of several women directors - two of the others being Rosanne Hunter and Yvonne Fletcher. Throughout the war they made educational films, mainly concerned with agriculture. Later she worked on a series of medical films aimed at trainee GPs and sponsored by ICI. 'I had no medical background, but I had a degree in zoology, so I was used to the discipline of research. I loved it.' From then on she freelanced, making documentaries, including three on mental hospitals, which she found fascinating, and several on deprived children - a poignant experience. 'I love freelancing and never had any problems getting work from the 1940s to the 1960s. It got more difficult as I got older. It's a young person's life. You have to be confident and optimistic and healthy.' She was on the point of retiring when she was offered a new lease of life - a series of film strips for the Coal Board explaining to miners the medical background to first-aid procedures. It lasted for years; by the time it was finished she was 67 and 'didn't want to hassle any more', so she retired and took up painting instead.

It was also during the war that Margaret Thomson became involved with the union, having been introduced to ACT by Frances Cockburn of Gaumont-British in the early 1940s. 'It's difficult to be a freelance and a trade unionist, but I was at Realist for some time. There were about eight of us, and we took it in turns to be shop steward. Very democratic, but there wasn't much for us to do, apart from sorting out the odd anomaly here and there.' Margaret Thomson's attitude to the union is very much like her attitude to feminism - she hasn't been very active, but she is all for it.

Although she agreed that it was more difficult for women to get jobs, and added that it would be for a hell of a long time to come, she wasn't sure that being a woman had made any difference to her colleagues' attitudes towards her. 'What made more of a difference was the ability to get on with people. If you could, you worked. If you couldn't, you didn't.' She describes herself as a shy woman, capable of being firm - which may be the reason she only struck real antagonism once or twice. There was the cameraman who would position his camera as directed and then persist in moving it back to his preferred position once shooting had started. There was the producer who asked to see her and, when she came into his office, went on reading his newspaper - she got hers out as well. But these were minor incidents. The major injustice has always been the lack of any real equality of opportunity for women. 'Yes', Margaret Thomson says with quiet conviction, 'I'm all for positive discrimination'.

Margaret Thomson
'I fell into directing early on', says Margaret Thomson, 'but it was disastrous and I had to go away and learn my trade'. It was during the war that she got the opportunity to do so - script-writing and directing, and always working as a freelance. 'It was a hard time, but I have

'The meetings were always packed, but no one would stand, so I said perhaps I should offer to stand, and then all the blokes would say, we don't want that stupid so-and-so, and someone else would come forward. I stood at the back and shouted, "All right, Mr Chairman, I'll stand". You could have heard a pin drop. I hadn't a clue and had never even looked at an agreement, but they voted me in.'

And no one else ever came forward. Monica Toye's male colleagues were nice to her - patronising, but nice. Management bullied her, shouted and swore at her. But very soon she got a chance to prove herself.

Monica Toye

Monica Toye comes from a very different area of the activities covered by ACTT - the labs. Less glamorous, perhaps, but often referred to as the backbone of the union. Described by former ACTT Organiser Bessie Bond as 'a marvellous shop steward, out of this world, a natural', Monica Toye has almost total recall of the events that led up to her being the first woman in the union to fill that particular role. It all started during the laboratory lock-out of 1954, when she had been at Denham for four to five years.

'It was a lovely atmosphere there, about 200 people. I didn't know anything about unions at the time. I was a bit flighty, I suppose, with long hair and sun dresses and liked the boys. During the lock-out I went to a meeting, just to listen. When they went back to work, it really disgusted me what they got. Differentials were introduced and the whole atmosphere changed. At the time we were also changing over to colour and there were running battles with management. Our shop steward fell ill and resigned. Some people set up a guild, which was anti-union, a sort of secret society. They asked me to join, but I wouldn't. However ignorant I was, I knew that was wrong. People were saying that if we didn't get a shop steward soon, the guild would take over.

Right ACTT Women's Conference.

'I'd been in the job for about three weeks when they called me up because a man was going to get the sack - for smoking. They were going to make an example of him. I asked to speak to him, right there in front of them all. He was one of our best printers, did all the experimental work. He'd been there 20 years and never been in any trouble before. I said they couldn't judge a man on one incident, they couldn't lose one of their best workers out of pique, and anyway management used to go up the carpenter's shop to smoke as well. That put the cat among the pigeons. But, anyway, they didn't sack him. Everyone rallied round me. They thought I'd done it.

'After that, I thought, that union agreement will be my Bible, and I learned it off by heart - literally. We got a lot of things done - rates for colour, protective clothing, compensation for dermatitis, rates for advertisements, and we used to black work when producers wouldn't pay. It's not emphasized enough that it's the union that does these things. There are so many hard-working trade union officials who never get any credit. The people at the top don't emphasize it enough - they're too keen on getting involved in national or world events. Much as I respect that, I think they've got out of touch with the man on the shop floor.'

That keeping in touch is hard work,

Above Women in broadcasting discussing positive action for equal opportunities. ACTT's Committee on Equality collaborates with the Black Media Workers Association in combating discrimination in the film and broadcasting industries.

Monica Toye herself can vouch. She had her own job all the time she was shop steward and for the six years she was Vice-President, sometimes worked a 66-hour week. It was hard going too, she admits, keeping up with the men, especially with all that drinking. 'Women can't take it. But you have to be there, because often the most important business is done in the pub after the meeting.' Otherwise, women are capable of doing anything - if they want to. 'Women have got to be prepared to give up more of their time, whatever their domestic commitments.' Creches and childcare arrangements would help but, as Monica Toye sees it, women simply don't want to get involved in union work. 'It can be fantastic, such good fun. But no one ever tells you that. The image is all wrong and doesn't attract young people.'

Any sort of separatism or favourable treatment for women is also wrong. 'When I was there, we said we wouldn't go to the Women's TUC because it meant segregation, and it had no power. It was just a sop. But now they're going again. Daphne Ancell says it's good training-ground, you gain confidence and you meet other women. But I think it's cutting off their noses to spite their faces. As to equality of opportunity, you can't have legislation to say you're good enough for a job. It's wrong, and so are quotas. It won't do women any good.'

Bessie Bond

Bessie Bond, ACTT Organiser for over 20 years, is of a similar opinion. 'I hope', she says, 'that you're not going to write a feminist piece'.

Born in Glasgow and brought up by a widowed mother (her father died of TB at the horrifyingly early age of 28) she left school at the age of 14 (on a Friday) and went to work in a factory (on the following Monday). There, and later in London, she became involved in trade union work. But it wasn't until the war years that she became a full-time trade union employee, with ACT. She had taught herself to type, had had the odd

office job here and there, and started out as a general factotum. A few months later she became one of the two national organisers. 'Not a woman's organiser', she emphasizes.

At the time, 'wages and hours of work were appalling and there was no paid overtime'. Bessie Bond was attached in turn to various sections - Editorial, the Labs ('I loved the Labs, the proletariat'), Shorts and Documentaries ('I adored Shorts and Docs'), Publicity and Stills. 'I was very good at getting people to work, drawing them in as stewards or committee members. Most of them became friends. Some of them have been my friends for 40 years. All my friends are film people, all my intimate friends.' It is clear that, despite her reputation for toughness, she has always been very popular, not just within the union but with management as well. 'They all called me Bessie and the bottle would come out. Maybe they hated my guts, but they were so relieved to discover I wasn't actually an ogre.' She had many a battle with one company which wouldn't allow shop stewards into meetings, leaving her to negotiate on her own. 'But I would always go back to the members. I would never settle anything there and then.'

'Of course it's a tough job and very few women do it. It's physically tough as well as intellectually demanding, and you need to be resilient. You were always dealing with men, which made you very, very vulnerable, and you had to be careful. Some of them thought you were a bit easy. But I always had my feet on the ground. We used to get the odd bottle of Scotch or perfume, but I was reluctant to accept any other gifts from employers.'

She describes the business of negotiating as 'thrilling - I absolutely loved it'. Hard going at first, it started to get easier as the union grew, but 'there was always a sticky company you had to battle with, and the worst were the fly-by-nights doing commercials. They were absolute bastards'. Others were more friendly and respectful, one employer going so far as to ask her advice about his wayward son, because he considered her to be a 'wise woman'.

She insists that she never experienced any discrimination. 'A lot of these feminist issues are exaggerated. I can see the necessity of providing creches for union conferences, perhaps, but otherwise the whole business is overdone. I've come across much more racial prejudice than discrimination against women, and of course the union should be fighting both. But there's no need for a special officer. All the organisers should be fighting injustice wherever they find it. I did. That's what trade unionism is all about.'

Neither Bessie Bond nor any of the other women I have mentioned so far have any children, although Margaret Thomson acquired a stepson late in life and is now a grandmother. Although none of them cited childlessness as a deliberate choice made in order to further a career, they all admitted that they might not have been able to achieve what they had in conjunction with motherhood. Might, not would. I got the impression that motherhood simply wasn't an issue, and that the tacit assumption was that the exiguous demands of working within the industry, especially as a freelance, automatically rendered the whole question irrelevant. I doubt if there are many women working today who would feel the same. Largely because of the women's movement (circa early 1970s) women are no longer content to make tacit assumptions, whether about children,

choice of career or availability of opportunities. On the contrary, these questions are agonised over, not just privately, but collectively. Although much has been achieved in recent years, the younger women I spoke to were, paradoxically, far less sanguine about either the industry as a whole or the place of women within it, than were their predecessors.

Sarah Boston
Sarah Boston, director and at one time ACTT's only-ever pregnant Vice-President, finds the question of motherhood central to any thinking about women and television.

'When I was at Granada in the 1960s, there was only one woman in an important job who had children. If the others had any, they managed to conceal the fact. When I used an all-woman crew in 1976, quite a few of us had children. This was the change over ten years. But it's still a problem for some women. If it's a matter of free choice, then that's OK, but so often women feel they can't have children if they're going to work in television. It is difficult. But it's not impossible. One of the things that makes up your mind for you is seeing other women who do have kids. Directing is draining work, and it's difficult to come home after a day of it and spend time with my daughter. But it's good for you. At work you get used to people doing what you want them to. That doesn't work with a six-year-old. And of course I never take on any work that's going to take me away from home for days or weeks on end. Some compromises have to be made.'

Sarah Boston graduated from Sussex University in the 1960s, 'those halcyon days of high employment'. She got a job at Granada as a researcher on a local programme - a good salary and a rolling contract. She had no particular ambition to work in television and quickly became disillusioned with the magazine format which 'essentially trivialised everything'. After two and a half years she was allowed, by virtue of a local agreement, to direct a 25-minute documentary, but told afterwards that she had to stay on as a researcher. 'A job came up as a director and I knew I wouldn't get it, partially because they'd taken on a woman the year before as a trainee director. And I was a bit too stroppy, a bit too critical.' She was right. When she didn't get the job, she left Granada and went to the local labour exchange. Things happened slowly after that, with a few breaks here and there, mainly from the BBC. It wasn't until she'd made her own first documentary that she decided this was what she really wanted to do.

Below Leeds Animation Workshop members with the £1,000 that Leeds City Council donated to their collective.

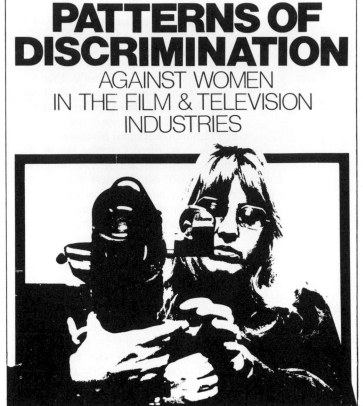

PATTERNS OF DISCRIMINATION
AGAINST WOMEN IN THE FILM & TELEVISION INDUSTRIES

Above The major report drawn up for ACTT in 1975 by Sarah Benton and others.

'At last I had an ambition. But the more I knew what I wanted, the harder it became to get it. I'm not interested in television for the sake of television, but for the opportunity to say certain things. All my films are based on allowing people to talk about their own lives without the mediation of a narrator or any form of commentary. I've made quite a few films about women, but not all. Rather, they come out of a feminist consciousness. When I filmed a mining community, I allowed the miners' wives as much time as the miners themselves. There was almost nothing explicit in the whole film. It was just taken for granted that women were of equal importance. I think that can change people's consciousness, whether the group is women, blacks or handicapped people.' Books can (let's hope) serve the same function, and Sarah Boston has written two - one on the life and death of her own Down's Syndrome baby; the other, *Women Workers and Trade Unions*, published in 1981.

In the early 1970s she was active on the ACTT Committee on Equality, which was responsible for the report, *Patterns of Discrimination*, published in 1975. What emerged from that report was incontrovertible evidence of discrimination against women, not only in film and television, but in the laboratories as well. The main problems were - it was difficult or impossible for women to move into certain grades; there were few

opportunities for training; and childcare facilities and maternity leave were both rarities. 'Resolutions were put forward at Annual Conference, but nothing happened. The push had come from a group of women at the top in London and had never got through to the grassroots. It was only three years or so later that the women at Granada started agitating, and there came a groundswell of anger from women on the shop floor up and down the country.'

Lyn Lloyd

Lyn Lloyd was the person mainly responsible for the agitation at Granada. At the time of the report she was working as an assistant film librarian and could see what was happening at local level - women were not progressing and were ghettoised. When there appeared to be no action as a result of the report she decided to become active in the union, and eventually became a shop steward.

'I tried to get a women's group together across the unions - the others were ETU, NATTKE and NUJ — but we had a really hard time even getting meetings off the ground. We'd put notices on the boards and the men would deface them, so we ended up putting them in the ladies' loos. The first meeting was amazing with women standing up and making all sorts of revelations. We got a creche campaign going, but basically the group fizzled out. We had no power. Management wouldn't negotiate with us because we weren't a union. So we decided we all had to go away and work through our own shops.'

It was only after fighting as a shop steward for other issues within the union that Lyn Lloyd felt she gained enough confidence from her colleagues at national level to ask for a Women's Conference. What emerged from the conference was that there was a gap - on the one hand, there was the Equality Committee, who had produced the report, but felt they had no support at local level; on the other, there were the women in the regions, who knew what was going on but felt powerless to act, and were very angry. 'There was this euphoric feeling of, at last we're together'. Conference decided that the Equality Committee, previously

elected from the General Council, should also include regional representatives. And it passed a unanimous motion to be taken to Annual Conference - that there should be an Equality Officer.

'We wanted someone professional because we were all doing jobs. We didn't think the motion would get through Annual Conference, and we had to organise ourselves before conference. I proposed it because I was known as a shop steward and not one of those middle-class feminists. This was an appeal to the Labs where they're all good trade unionists. We had a man to second it and a black woman to speak to the motion and show that racism was involved as well. We'd managed to counter opposition from officials at national level, who'd felt that the appointment was some sort of criticism of them.'

Once the motion had been passed and Sandra Horne appointed, a second Women's Conference was held that aimed to get her brief together. 'At the end of that we decided we had to get someone in to support Sandra. She has to deal with an all-male Executive and nearly all male organisers. And there are a lot of racists in the union. Trying to get black people in is worse than trying to protect women.' The conference taught women how to deal with meetings, how to get items on to or moved up an agenda, and how to 'wheeler-deal' with other sections in order to get support. In short, how to be trade unionists? 'Yes, but also how to con people and play the man's game. I'm afraid it's still necessary. The only way you can change things is through the trade unions. When I left Granada, 60 per cent of editors' assistants were women, whereas before it had been a 100 per cent men. We also got the company to bring in women engineers and camerawomen. That's the sort of thing a woman shop steward can do. I've now been elected to the Executive as a Vice-President, and I hope other, younger women are going to follow suit.

Below Jan Mathew (left) greets Milena Canonero — Oscar winner for the costume design of *Chariots of Fire* — at the 1982 Annual Conference.

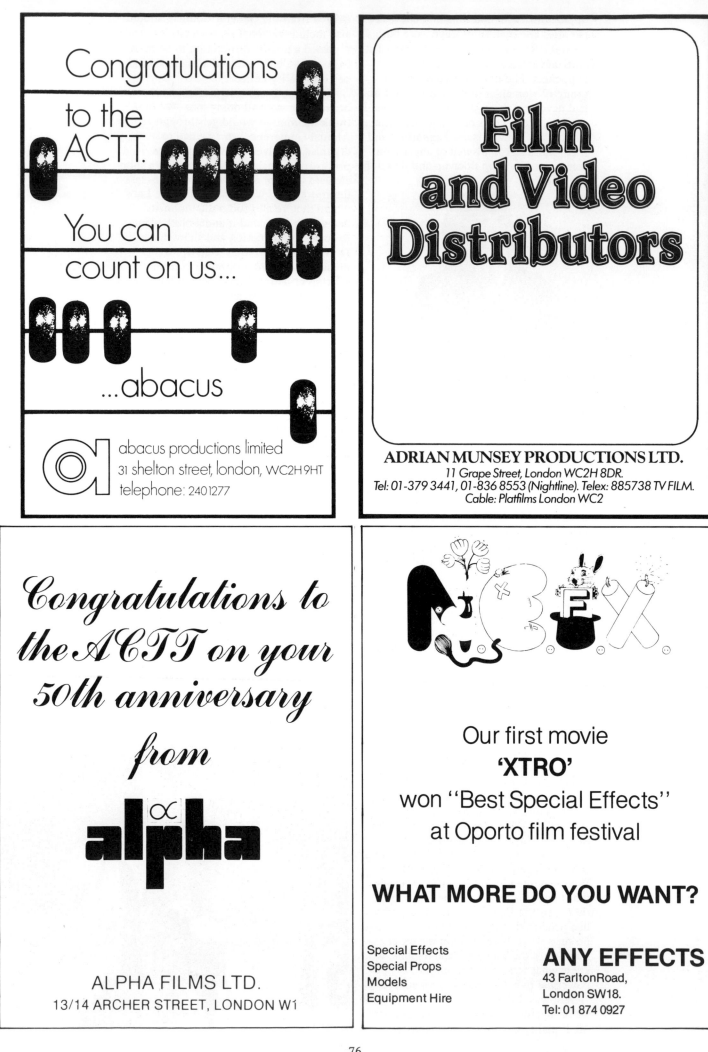

We need to ensure that there are always some women in positions of power.'

Sandra Horne

The Equality Officer, Sandra Horne, appointed in January 1982, has now found her feet in the industry. The job is beset with difficulties, as much within the union itself as in its dealings with management.

Above Sandra Horne (right) with Jan Mathew.

'Some of the women say that any woman can make it - it's just a matter of effort. Others say, oh yes, but we really think the conditions for us making it are somewhat different.' This latter is Sandra Horne's view and accords with the principle of positive discrimination. As to the men, some are supportive, some don't see what it's all about and others are actively opposed. 'It would be unrealistic to expect any group which has power to relinquish it willingly. If we were running things, would we say it? "You've got where you are because you have been discriminated in favour of?". It's not an argument that's easy to accept.' Because ACTT has, generally speaking, a good record, people tend to feel criticised and threatened if an Equality Officer says, 'All is not well here'. Sandra Horne admits that, in a way, this is a criticism, 'But, on the other hand, people tend to respond to pressures that are put on them'. Sometimes the difficulty

is getting equality matters discussed at all. 'You talk about the pay claim, and you talk about equality when there's time - which there never is, of course.'

At the moment the Equality Officer is negotiating with television companies individually, with employers in the film industry at national level, and is just getting started in the Labs. ITCA has agreed to 'desex' the national agreement, and to improve the maternity clause. Not that all managements can see the point. The managing director of one TV company told Sandra Horne that, of course, women can have equal opportunities if they make a choice - children or a career. 'So I said to him, "Have you got any children?" And when he said yes, I said, "Don't you think there's a flaw in your argument somewhere?" But I don't think he knew what I was talking about.'

The recession doesn't help matters - not only have the spurious arguments of those who advocate that women should stay at home been given some credibility because they are endorsed by cabinet ministers, but 'in times of high unemployment, it's very difficult to say to a TV company, we want you to bring in 25 black apprentices now'.

What does Sandra Horne expect from the job? 'A miracle? I've taken up the job when there's a certain impetus anyway. My job is to see that the union has some control over that impetus so that developments happen in a way that doesn't undermine collective agreements, etc. Not to let that impetus go in a vague and woolly direction with one token woman and black everywhere, and one male PA. To keep it all going at some recognisable speed. The trouble is that this union is only 20 per cent women, so you can't turn out the vote and win, like you could in NALGO. If the men don't want positive discrimination, it won't happen. And that's called democracy so it will take effort and commitment at all levels.'

Right ACTT Annual Conference 1983. New Executive Committee members (from left to right) Joanne Gooding, Jan Mathew, Bianka Dadswell and Jenny Wilkes.

WE'D NEVER HAVE MADE THEM WITHOUT YOU!

In recent years, Euston Films has produced some of the most popular film drama on television including <u>The Sweeney</u>, <u>Out</u>, <u>Danger UXB</u>, <u>The Knowledge</u>, <u>Charlie Muffin</u>, <u>The Flame Trees of Thika</u>, <u>Minder</u>, and <u>Widows</u>.

Later this year sees the transmission of <u>Reilly</u>, a twelve episode series on the life and times of masterspy Sidney Reilly, a legend in his own era.

Such successes would not have been achieved without the professionalism of ACTT members. Euston Films congratulates ACTT on its 50th anniversary and looks forward to the support of ACTT members on future productions.

Danger UXB

EUSTON FILMS

The Sweeney

ACT FILMS LIMITED

*R*alph Bond tells the story of the only film company owned by a union. And Richard Gates, his successor as Honorary Consultant, looks ahead.

The late 1940s and 1950s were bad times for British film production. Few films were being made, and there was mass unemployment among film technicians. The crisis was the main subject of debate within the union and one of the suggestions put forward at the Annual General Meeting in 1949 was that we should set up our own film production company. And so it was that ACT Films Limited was established in 1950 with three main objectives − to make hundred per cent British films; to give work to unemployed ACT members; and to prove that films of quality could be made on reasonable budgets while observing all the appropriate union agreements.

The first directors of the new company were nominated by the General Council. They were Anthony Asquith (Chairman), Charles Wheeler (Vice-Chairman) and

Above Ralph Bond, doyen of ACT Films. **Right** Richard Attenborough in *The Man Upstairs.*

Robert Asher, W R Brinton, Desmond Dickinson, George Elvin, 'Sash' Fisher, Frank Fuller, J F Harris, K J Horne, R J Minney, Sidney Cole, Ken Gordon and myself. The Board was fortunate in having as its secretary Mr T S Stallabrass of the firm of solicitors Pollard, Stallabrass & Co. Mr P C Samuel was appointed as Manager and Executive Producer, and offices were secured in Victoria Street. The Board appointed a Finance and General Purposes Committee composed of a number of the directors and the Secretary to get things off the ground, but it was decided that the company would be registered as a non-profit making organisation, with any incidental profits going to the union's benevolent fund.

ACT Films Ltd's formation was made possible through the support and influence of Harold Wilson MP, who was then the President of the Board of Trade. He welcomed the project and urged the recently established National Film Finance Corporation to help finance our first film. This was a feature production called *Green Grow the Rushes*. After some rather difficult negotiations, the NFFC agreed to put up approximately two-thirds of the budget and the Co-operative Wholesale Society Bank put up the remainder. Production started in June 1950, with filming mainly at Romney Marsh on location and at Elstree Studios for interiors. The star of the film was a relatively unknown actor by the name of Richard Burton, although Phil Samuel was astute enough to forecast that that particular lad would go far. *Green Grow the Rushes* was completed £4,000 under the budget of £100,000. British Lion agreed to be its distributors and it was delivered to them in November 1950. Then the trouble started.

There was a great deal of hostility towards ACT at that time on the part of exhibitors and the big circuits, because of the union's outspoken attacks on them for their contribution to the contemporary crisis in the British film industry. Accordingly, the two major circuits refused to book our film. At that time it was possible to appeal against such a decision through the Board of Trade, who had appointed a selection committee with powers to make an order requiring any film to be shown on one of the principal circuits. No such order was made, however, and eventually British Lion presented the film at a trade show and set about getting as many bookings as possible from independent exhibitors.

Then another unfortunate event occurred. The film critic of a daily newspaper smuggled himself into the trade show and wrote a hostile review in his paper. The resulting adverse hostility was not alleviated by the dishonest circumstances under which the review had

been written. In the end, the film received a few hundred bookings but failed to recover its production costs. The technicians who had worked on the film were to get a share in any profits, but they got none. There is a lesson somewhere in that experience.

The disappointing reception of *Green Grow the Rushes* was a severe setback to the new company, but fortunately all distributors did not share the prejudices we had encountered and Bill Gell of Monarch Films commissioned the company to make a series of second features, which enjoyed considerable success. There was a demand then for second features because most cinemas ran double bills and we welcomed the chance to make them because they often provided launching opportunities and good experience for unemployed or young film technicians.

But there were headaches, as some Board minutes of 1952 recall. 'When it is realised that ACT Films, Monarch Films, Lloyds Bank and the guarantors of completion had to pass the story first, and then the script, to say nothing of the Censor, the difficulties in doing these subjects cannot be imagined.' The films had to be closely budgeted and scheduled. Their average cost was £14-15,000 and the maximum shooting time was three weeks. Almost all of them were succesful in recovering their costs and showing small profits. There were, of course, far more cinemas than there are today. To give a few examples, *Night was our Friend* secured 1,335 bookings, *Private Information* 1,364, *Circumstantial Evidence* 1,568, *Dangerous Cargo* 1,196, *House of Blackmail* 1,191. Altogether, we made 12 second features between 1951 and 1962. By this time Phil Samuel had retired from ACT Films and Henry Passmore replaced him as manager, successfully leading the company until he too retired in March 1954. I was appointed by the Board to succeed him.

ACT Films was, of course, anxious to make more first features with bigger budgets and more shooting time. The opportunity came in 1952 when Terence Rattigan offered us his script for *The Final*

Right Honor Blackman and Richard Burton in the fairground scene of *Green Grow the Rushes*.

Test with Anthony Asquith directing, and finance and distribution through the Rank Organisation. R J Minney was appointed as producer and the stars were Jack Warner and Robert Morley. This was probably the first British feature film with a story involving the national game of cricket. *The Final Test's* art director had been unemployed on account of being allegedly too old for work. But the job he did on this ACT Films production proved his former employers wrong, and fulfilled one of our original objectives in setting up the company - to give members opportunities being denied them elsewhere in the industry. *The Final Test* came in at £86,000 and had a full release on the Rank circuit, but all our efforts to

get Rank to re-issue the film when the next test series was played in England were to no avail.

In 1958 a talented young documentary scriptwriter, Alun Falconer, came to us with an interesting outline for a feature film. The NFFC liked it, too, and Alun was commissioned to write a full script. British Lion agreed to part finance and distribute the film, which became *The Man Upstairs.* British Lion suggested that Richard Attenborough should play the leading part, which he did to perfection.

We asked Don Chaffey, a promising young director who had not had the breaks he deserved, to direct and he turned in a first-class job. *The Man Upstairs* was shot on location and at Shepperton Studios. It was produced by

Bob Dunbar, and it came in under budget.

Another useful commission came in 1961 from the Children's Film Foundation. We made *The Piper's Tune* for them, shot almost entirely on location in Wales. This film was received with enthusiasm and justified all the hard work put into it by the crew, headed by Muriel Box as director. Our next feature film was

Don't Panic Chaps! which was based on a radio play and appealed to us as an anti-war comedy. Hammer Films liked it and agreed to put up the money and distribute through Columbia. This film was almost entirely shot on location in the west of England, and it achieved a very successful full circuit booking, followed by television sales here and in the USA, yielding a nice profit for all concerned.

In 1961 Arnold Wesker had written a play called *The Kitchen,* which had received considerable acclaim at the Royal Court Theatre. Arnold Wesker was interested in a screenplay for *The Kitchen,* which had been written by Sidney Cole.

We took the project to the NFFC who agreed to put up the total budget (under £30,000). This was the first time that the NFFC had agreed to wholly finance an ACT film and they had no cause to regret that decision. Again, we were able to give a chance to a young director, James Hill, who had made his name in documentaries. A set was constructed at Shepperton Studios and the combination of Arnold Wesker, James Hill and Sidney Cole resulted in a successful film.

By the mid-1960s the position of independent film producers was bleak. The financial position of ACT Films reflected that climate and was extremely depressing because it had always been a basic principle that we should survive financially on our own and never seek money from our union. This we adhered to rigidly (except for one small loan which was quickly repaid). By 1965 the situation had not improved and so I offered to step down as a paid general manager. The Board accepted my offer and I carried on looking after the affairs of the company as an unpaid honorary consultant.

Throughout its history, ACT Films had been hoping to persuade the labour movement and the trade unions to utilise the film medium for their own purposes and interests. We tried to set up a film about the *Tolpuddle Martyrs*, but no one was interested. We tried to raise money for a film of *The Ragged Trousered Philanthropists*, Robert Tressell's great book, which had been dramatised at the Unity Theatre. No dice. Then we submitted an extensive outline to the Labour Party on its history and policies. Again, with no success. It was not until 1969 that the Amalgamated Engineering Union (as it then was) commissioned us to make a documentary. This was a real breakthrough. Alun Falconer was asked to write the script, while Ewan McColl wrote and sang a marvellous theme song. *We are the Engineers* was received with enthusiasm by the AEU's Executive and up to 20 copies of the film were kept in continuous circulation for several years. The film was shown in every region and AEU members who rarely attended branch meetings came to see the film and learn about their union's history and traditions.

Two years later, in 1971, Jack Jones, the General Secretary of the Transport and General Workers' Union, asked us to make a film for an important union anniversary. This was called *One in Five* and premiered to a packed audience at the Royal Festival Hall. But, despite the success of these two documentaries, no other unions responded to our initiatives. 1981 was the year of the People's March for Jobs, starting from Liverpool and gradually embracing every district in the country on its long trek to London. ACT Films immediately decided that this historic event should be recorded on film, and scores of ACTT members enthusiastically volunteered their services. All agreed to work on a voluntary basis, as their contribution to the fight against unemployment. Many service companies in the industry also offered help. So the actual cost of the film was kept low, and the money was raised from donations from trade unions and ACTT members. *The People's March* successfully captured the spirit of the march. The voices heard were the voices of those participating, and the music was the music played on the march and at the great welcoming gala in London. The film was in great demand within the labour movement and it covered all of its distribution costs.

During the 30 years of its existence, ACT Films Ltd has given work to almost a thousand unemployed members, and has made a useful contribution to British film production at times of crisis. The experience convinced me that we have the finest craftsmen, technicians, actors, directors and facilities in the world.

The future of ACT Films

The future for any production company is always difficult to predict with any certainty and this is no less true for ACT Films. However, with new blood on the board, the company is looking at the ways in which film-making has changed in the last decade and trying to move with the changes.

This is particularly true for TV outlets and the production of video tapes for unions, where in the past they might have had a 16mm documentary. ACT Films is also exploring the Grant Aided Sector, in an effort to have a small permanent unit available to record important events in the trade union movement as they occur.

This does not mean that ACT Films intends to ignore the traditional areas of film-making, but that, in the light of the current state of the industry, the company expects to change the emphasis of its productions, with one of the chief aims being to give work to members.

With these thoughts in mind, ACT Films hopes to have at least another 30 successful years ahead.

Above Richard Gates, ACT Film's Honorary Consultant since 1983, confers with his predecessor.

UNIVERSAL PICTURES LIMITED
139 PICCADILLY, LONDON W1V 9FH

METHOD SCHOOLS

Anthony Asquith, ACTT's first President, delivered this lecture in 1939. It remains as a tribute to him.

To go right back to the beginning of films, I think the thing that really fascinated us was just the fact that the pictures moved at all. To see a man eating an apple pie was a marvellous experience, and if, after he had eaten the apple pie, the process was reversed and the pie came out of his mouth and became whole again, our joy was complete. Movement continued to be the prime factor in the early pictures, of which I think the Westerns were the most popular type. All that was necessary for a time was for a beautiful heroine to fall into the clutches of a villain, usually recognisable by his twirled moustaches, and to be rescued at the last minute by the hero.

Below Encounter between two maestros: Alfred Hitchcock and Anthony Asquith.

'Fifty years? The first fifty, I tell you, is only the start. The best is yet to come'

-Henry Ford

Henry wasn't always right - but this time we couldn't agree more.

Here's to the hundred!

Tyburn Productions Limited

PINEWOOD STUDIOS · IVER HEATH · BUCKINGHAMSHIRE
TELEPHONE: IVER 651 700   TELEX: 847505

Well, after a time this type of action picture began to lose interest with the audience and it was found necessary to make the actors more real to the audience and so hold their interest. It was about this time that D W Griffith invented the 'close-up' and this, of course, immediately established a new and more intimate relationship between the actor and the audience.

The silent days

In the silent days if a director wished to convey an emotion to the audience what he did was to take a large close-up of the heroine registering a violent emotion, fear maybe, and then if his leading lady was not adequate to her task he put in a title which described exactly what the heroine was feeling. The limitations of this are

Above *A Woman of Paris.* **Centre** *Intolerance.* **Below** *Cabinet of Dr Caligari.*

obvious, and I think that it is to the German cinema that we owe the next great step, which is seeing not only the heroine being frightened but also what is frightening her, and by tricks of staging and lighting, such as double exposure, making that appear frightening to us. The Germans, then, were the first to show in a film what was happening from the point of view of the actors in the film.

To take an actual example, you will probably all remember the famous film *Cabinet of Dr Caligari*. The film opens with a shot of a perfectly ordinary garden through which a man is walking. He sits down on a perfectly ordinary garden seat and gets into conversation with his neighbour. The film then takes up the thread of the conversation and we are transported to a completely unreal town where the streets are crooked, the houses set all askew and so on, until we finally realise that the story is going on in the mind of a madman. And at the end it is

revealed that the characters in the story are merely the hallucinations of a lunatic based on the doctor and other figures in the asylum where he is being kept.

The next advance was, I think, made by Chaplin in his film *A Woman of Paris* and there is one incident in that which illustrates very well what I mean. A boy and a girl have been childhood friends and wish to marry but their parents will not allow it. Years after they meet again in Paris and the man goes home to the woman's luxurious apartment. In the middle of their conversation the woman opens a drawer and a man's collar falls out. There is a rather embarrassed silence and then they take up the conversation where it left off. In this way Chaplin has perfectly expressed the shock of disillusionment of the man when he discovers that his friend is being kept by another man, and the way in which a man would naturally hide his embarrassment and carry on as if nothing had happened.

This naturalism is far removed from the way such a scene would have been treated before.

We can all imagine the dramatic attitude that would have been struck at the discovery. As another example of the way in which Chaplin used his shots economically for building up an atmosphere and building the story is his

ADVENTURE AND EXPLORATION

Dudh Kosi
France, Paris Festival of Sport – Grand Prix du Festival. La Plagne Festival – Grand Prix du Festival and – Film Journalists Jury Award.
Canada, Banff Mountaineering Festival – Best Film of the Festival and Best Outdoor Film.
Yugoslavia, Kranj Festival of Sport – Silver Triglav, Best Camera Award and Pierre de Courbertin Prize.
Switzerland, Les Diablerets Film Festival – Diable D'Or and Prix du Public.
Italy, Trento Mountaineering Festival – Best Photography Award.
U.S.A, International Emmy Awards, New York – Emmy Award Nominee.
U.S.A., Telluride Mountainfilm Festival – Adventure Class Award.
Spain, San Sebastian Mountainfilm Festival – Award of Honour for best film on mountain sports.

Everest Unmasked
Italy, Trento Mountaineering Festival – Silver Gentian Award.
USA, Telluride Film Festival, Colorado – Best film on expeditionary mountaineering. Spain, San Sebastion Mountaineering Film Festival – Popular Vote Prize.

Matterhorn
Italy, Les Diablerets Film Festival – Grand Prix.
USA, Telluride Mountainfilm Festival – Award.

The Cerro Torre Enigma
Colorado, Telluride Mountaineering Film Festival – Best Film on Mountaineering.
Canada, Banff Festival of Mountaineering Film – Grand Prize of the Festival and Best Historical Mountaineering Film.

We are pleased to have made our own contribution to the success of ITV over the last 15 years.

Filming the Impossible
London, Travel and Sport Film Festival – Silver Prize in the Sport Section.
Italy, The Trento Film Festival – Silver Gentian Award for the Best Documentary film.
New York Film Festival Silver Medal 1982

DRAMA

Thick as Thieves
Pye Oscar for the best regional production of 1972.
Item
ITV drama entry Monte Carlo 1974.
Machine Gunner Royal Television Society drama award 1976.
Anthony Purdy
ITV entry Monte Carlo 1971.
Sir Ambrose Fleming Memorial Awards (For services to West Country Television) Alan Taylor, Terry Harding, Bruce Hockin.
Jangles ITV entry for the Prix Jeunesse, 1982.

DOCUMENTARIES

The First Robin Cousins
– Royal Television Society Award 1978.
It's a Dogs's Life
– Royal Television Society Award 1979.
The World of Frank Letch
– Asian Broadcasting Union Prize.
Scars – Gold Award International Cinema Festival, Nyon.
The Basques
– portrait of a people –
Best Film Award

NEWS

Report West
Three times winner of Royal Television Society awards for best regional news films.
Report Wales
British TV News Film Award 1970
Cameraman of the Year – Hard news – Frank Bevan

OPERA

A Christmas Carol
Salzburg Festival Opera Prize 1980

CHILDRENS

Arthur of the Britons
Writers Guild of Great Britain best children's drama script of 1974.
King of the Castle
Nominated for a British Academy Drama Award 1978.
Flower Stories
Barcelona Festival Award for animation programmes 1972.

RELIGION

There Go I
Unda Festival Award for religious programmes 1972.

The coming of sound

Just as the Germans made the camera see through the eye of the actor, so with sound we can make the audience hear what the character is saying. To take a well-known example. In Hitchcock's early talkie, *Blackmail,* a girl has murdered a

the first time to a close shot of the girl on the floor at the side of the stage. The music starts again with a long glissando on the harp and three chords for full orchestra. On the glissando the girl gets up. On the first chord she catches sight of the young man and we cut to a close-up of

Above Alfred Hitchcock directing *The 39 Steps* with Robert Donat and Madeleine Carroll.

man by stabbing him with a knife. (We don't seem to be able to get away from that knife). She goes down to lay the table for breakfast and a gossipy neighbour drops in. The neighbour, not knowing the situation of course, is full of talk about the murder, and as she continues, her voice becomes a blur of sound to the girl, out of which at frequent intervals the one word 'knife' stands out until at last when the girl has to pick up a bread knife she cannot bring herself to touch it.

Just as we have use of metaphors with a picture, so we have the use of sound metaphor. There is no reason, for instance, why in a quarrel with two men raising their voices in anger we should not cut to the sound of a machine gun or road drill. Indeed, the use of sound can help us over many of our problems. To take one example from a film I made, *Dance Little Lady,* taken from Compton Mackenzie's book *Carnival.* In the book, after the girl meets her boyfriend there is a very charmingly written series of love scenes in different parts of London.

To get the same effect I decided not to show a series of small love scenes but to treat it in an essentially film way. The girl is a ballet dancer and the boy is at a performance of the ballet (actually Tchaikovsky's *Lac des Cygnes).* The music comes to a pause and with it we come for

him. On the second chord we cut back to her, and on the third we cut back to him gazing at her. After that we had their meeting outside the theatre. Then the girl goes home. She runs into her room and throws up the window. As she does so we hear again the harp glissando and a mix then follows the 16 bars of music to which she has been dancing in the ballet.

On the first beat of every fourth bar I cut to a different shot. First, Hampstead Heath - mostly sky, a small clump of trees and a kite streaming across the picture with the two lovers walking arm-in-arm. Second, a rather misty long-shot looking down on London. Third, a churned-wake of a river steamer, which panning up reveals the two lovers seated in the stern of the steamer, with the four chimneys of Lots Road Power Station stark against the evening sky. The point of these shots was that they actually danced in time to the ballet music. I did convey, I hope, the effect of the lyrical love scenes in the book in a very small space.

Finally, I would like to pass on an anecdote told me by an esteemed friend who said to me the other day, "What's the use of the Ten Commandments - they only tell you what not to do and put ideas into your head". Well, if I have succeeded in putting a few ideas into your head I think perhaps this has been worthwhile.

91

UIP House. Beadon Rd. Hammersmith. London W.6. Tel: 01-741 9041

Wolf Rilla looks back with remembered
pleasure on three heady decades in the
history of British film-making and says
there are now more fascinating
ways of making films
than ever before.

The phone rang at 4.30
one Friday afternoon in
1952, and the producer
at the other end said
he'd got this feature,
starts shooting Monday
week, and his director had gone
and got the mumps. Was I by any chance
available? He knew damn well I was. Only days
before he'd shut the door politely in my face -
'I'll let you know if anything crops up, old
boy!' Now he said, 'I'll get the script to
you by special messenger. Have a read
and ring me at home tomorrow to
tell me whether you're interested'.
I could have told him there and
then. I didn't have to read the
script. I went through the
motions, but the truth is I'd
have directed the phonebook.
For more than a year I'd been
banging my head against those
firmly closed doors - 'Sorry old
boy, seen your work on
television of

Film-maker in wonderland

'Decline' is a word that now has a permanent place in the vocabulary of the cinema. Perhaps this is understandable. Are not the massed batallions of the American major studios faced with the disintegration of their traditional markets and all the financial losses that undoubtedly indicates? Is it not correct that in Britain, creative values aside, the climate for film-making is exceedingly arid, even with our recent Oscar successes? All these things are undoubtedly true, yet to label them 'decline' is to view films through the eyes of a recent, tortured past. I have no doubt that for some, what is happening will mean the end, but for many others there will be fresh beginnings and new opportunities. This is a period of transition, not atrophy, though God knows, both processes can be equally painful.

We need to grasp the nettle that the entire function and economic reality of cinemas is in the process of altering for ever in the English-speaking countries. From being the main, sometimes the only, source of return for films, cinemas are beginning to take their final step as a commercial enterprise, becoming what is in effect a promotional vehicle for films whose actual pay-off will be cable, cassette, satellite and off-air broadcasting.

What we must always bear in mind is that this shift does not represent a great sea change in the expectations of the majority of those who want to watch films.

My own view is that the 'blockbuster', as we know it, will not survive because it is a form that demands a budgetary level that represents simply too large a risk. But the mainstay of cinema will continue to be dramatic or 'narrative' films, and they will continue to be extremely popular. Don't take my word for it. Just look at the *Radio Times* or *TV Times* and see how films bought for television are scheduled. Watch how films are promoted in advance on the air. Television companies are as anxious to tell the public what feature films they have bought as to reveal what new programmes they have made themselves.

Once cinemas have undergone the change from being the main source of box-office revenue to being largely promotional vehicles, we could, to our amazement, find ourselves packing people in because it will have become comparatively cheap to see the films on show. The pay-off for the enthusiast who still attends will be the truly cinematic experience of seeing a film on a large screen, in darkness, with the best possible sound; and the pay-off for the industry will be a promotional fulcrum around which word of mouth will feed the interest of a mass audience of cable and satellite viewers.

From the audience's point of view, the medium will become more intimate. Even though television sets will become larger, they will not require the scale of image that the cinema screen demands. This may offend purists who believe that the framing of an image for the cinema is necessarily grander than that of a scene destined for television. But on the sort of budgets we are talking about we will find that film-making on the grand scale is a thing of the past. Furthermore, it is only by historical accident that television screens are square; I would not be at all surprised if the new generation of television screens changes in shape.

If there will not be a place for a director working on the scale of, say, David Lean, there will be more scope for the Ingmar Bergman or Ken Loach breed of film-maker. So films will not necessarily become trivialised. Efforts like the British Film Institute's regional theatres will become a more and more potent and important part of the cultural mix. But we must not be fooled

course, but movies - well, you need film credits before 'The Money' will take a chance on you. Come and see me again when you've done a film'. It was Catch-22. To get to direct a film you needed a credit, and to get a credit you needed to direct a film.

So here, at last, was my chance. An epic called *Noose For a Lady*. Schedule fifteen days, budget twelve thousand. And the producer, knowing how much I needed the credit, paid me peanuts - £150 for the job, I think; certainly less than the minimum rate for assistant directors, but of course there was no minimum for directors in 1952. Still, we were both taking chances. The sum total of my experience in film production was two visits to a film studio.

Ten days later, I stood on that stage at Merton Park Studios, where you had to build sets round the central stanchion, calling out my first 'Action!' with confidence I was far from feeling. I knew little, if anything, about the technical side of making movies. I didn't even know jargon that seemed familiar to the tea-boy. I had to work out as we went along what watching the overlap meant, or striking a flat, or cheating your eyeline, or direct reverses and over-shoulder complementaries. It was a tightrope act. I daren't admit to cast and crew how little I knew. But in a more fundamental sense I had the boundless confidence of youth, and the gamble paid off. Within a year of that first 'Action' I had directed four more pictures of the same kind - a rate of output I've never been able to match since. And one of the most important first lessons that I learnt was that a director is as good as his crew.

The fifties were a good period in which to start a career as a film director. Those second features - £12,000 to £15,000 three-week quickies - provided a marvellous training ground. It was, for a director, the equivalent of weekly rep. You learnt your craft the hard way - how to deliver the goods and entertain the customers no matter what the circumstances. And after a while you were ready to graduate - the actor to Shaftesbury Avenue or Broadway, the film director to Pinewood or Shepperton or Elstree. Both second features and weekly reps have all but disappeared. Perhaps something of a similar training is provided by television series with their ten-day turn-round - but such is the pressure there that they can rarely take a chance with an inexperienced hand.

There was a kind of innocent simplicity about the film industry in the fifties. It was compactly organised. There were basically two kinds of pictures - second and first features. There were three main production centres, and about 150 films were made every year. The threat of television and diminishing cinema

audiences was a cloud no bigger than a man's hand. The studio system was still more or less intact. As a director, your aim was a contract with Rank or ABPC or British Lion - the safety and continuity of in-house production.

Your idols, in whose footsteps you hoped to follow, were David Lean and Carol Reed. According to your temperament, you hoped to make pictures like *Great Expectations* or *The Third Man*. You might say that we were still in - albeit at the tail-end - the Augustan age of film making - traditional in form and content. It hadn't changed much since the heyday of the late thirties and forties. MGM - and the Man with the Gong - ruled. And the great impresario father figures - Alexander Korda and Michael Balcon - were still functioning. Your ambition was to come to the attention of such men.

My summons to present myself to John Grierson at the Great Western Hotel was almost as good. It came at the end of my first year as director. Grierson ran, in somewhat improbable tandem with John Baxter, an organisation known as Group Three, based at Beaconsfield Studios. This was the brain-child of Michael Balcon - a production centre established with the backing of the majors in order to provide an opportunity for new talent -

Top Right *Blow Up*. **Below** *The Third Man* and Wolf Rilla directing Diana Dors in *Rosie*.

directors, writers, actors - in a programme of modest budget, but not second feature type, films.

Grierson received me in his hotel room. He was in bed with a streaming cold, surrounded by scripts and cans of beer. He threw me one of the latter and, in his staccato Scots, fired off a salvo of questions. What kind of a film did I want to make? Why did I want to make films at all? What did I think of Rosselini and Italian Neorealism? Who was my favourite director? In the end he said, 'I suppose you'd better come and do something for us...'

I spent eighteen happy months at Group Three and made two-and-a-half films there. The half was an abortive musical for which we shot extensive tests with Petula Clark as a teenage soprano. I received press notices for the first time - 'that promising young director...'. One day I came out of a viewing theatre in Wardour Street to find Jimmy Lawrie (until shortly before the first managing director of the National Film Finance Corporation) waiting for me. He had this film, based on Arthur Grimble's *Pattern of Islands,* to be shot in Cinemascope (the first British Cinemascope film) entirely on location in the South Pacific. He thought I might like to have a go at it. And I thought I'd arrived in the Big League at last. But the banana skin is ever there, lying unsuspected in one's path....

For by the mid-fifties there were ominous rumbles. A slightly hysterical protesting-too-much note crept into promotional ballyhoos. *Pictures Are Better Than Ever* ran the preferred slogan. In Venice Diana Dors did her mink bikini act, and in Cannes starlets daringly bared their boobs to be embraced by Bob Mitchum on the beach. Rank embarked on its misguided and eventually disastrous policy of mid-Atlantic movies in a futile effort to break into the American market.

It has always been the practice in the film industry, whenever it runs into one of its perennial financial crises, to bang the big drum and shout louder than ever. But this time it was more than just another crisis. The very foundations were beginning to crack.

With the arrival of commercial television and the development of tape as a means of recording electronic images, the end of the film industry as we knew it had begun. By 1960, Korda was dead, and with him the particular era he had created. Ealing Studios, past its illustrious heyday, was sold to MGM. The brave experiment of Group Three was shut down for lack of funds. And a cold wind blew through the corridors of the big studios.

It wasn't only a question of escalating losses and diminishing attendances. Perhaps, though, because of these the search was on for new ways, artistically and commercially. To counter the threat of television, screens became wider and more gigantic. But, more important, the old established ways were being replaced by new forms, new approaches - new themes to be explored, new techniques to be applied. The iconoclastic wind of the *Nouvelle Vague* blew across the Channel, and a new generation of film makers - the Richardsons, Lindsay Andersons, John Schlesingers - began to beaver away amid the rumble of falling masonry.

And then, suddenly, we were in the sixties, in Swinging London, and the brief burgeoning Spring of the New Commercial Cinema with youth at the helm - the iconoclasts, the 'zoom-pow' boys, the wreckers and the innovators. When I started directing ten years earlier, in my thirties, a director under forty (with the exception of such wayward geniuses as Orson Welles) was practically unheard of. By the time I was half established in my early forties, the bearded boys of under 25

into believing that a romantic image of the cinema - which, incidentally, I share to my cost - can or must be maintained in the face of economic reality. The BFI's role as the cultural guardian of cinema as we know it should in many ways become easier as its brief becomes more clearly defined. This is one of the many areas that should receive an adequate level of subsidy from the cable system.

Television and cinema have evolved separately and differently; soon, not many miles down different roads, they must find a way to converge. Future film directors will be grounded in television and film finance will move in the same direction. Yet we are saddled, inadvertently, with anomalies that stand in our way. This is one reason why Channel 4 is so important - it could help to bring to an end a ridiculous situation in which freelance film-makers have effectively been prohibited from working in television.

Throw into this mix peripheral but important issues such as the video cassette market, and you realise that we have evolved to a point at which there is a sad lack of logic and common sense in the way both film and television are ordered. The most tragic consequence of the fact that some 70 per cent of all revenue from sales of video cassettes is accruing to what is in effect a 'black market' is not that 'valuable copyrights are being infringed' but rather that much of the money that the public pays to see films on cassette is not being recycled into the production system itself. This tight cycle of production finance is too poor to be able to afford leaks. That is a lesson the government might digest before considering throwing the cable networks open to companies that can be shown to have a less than firm commitment to production.

The next decade will be a roller-coaster for film-makers, with all the risks and excitement that that implies. I can only hope that the end of the division between film and television will serve to bring the realm of cinema entertainment closer to economic reality. At the same time, we must make absolutely sure that public-service broadcasting and those other institutions that contribute to our country's cultural output have access to the cable revenues that technology will release. I have no interest in supporting the creation of a new generation of media moguls, be they power-mad bureaucrats, faceless chairmen or voracious entrepreneurs. I want an industry in which the average well-made film, with reasonable success, offers an attractive return on investment. That will require discipline, which the cinema can and will learn from television. At the same time, television, through a closer relationship with the hurly-burly of the cinema industry, will do well to develop the necessary entrepreneurial skills that will be required if film-makers of all types are to be allowed to compete and survive in what is, whether we like it or not, an international industry. As I have said, we will learn from each other, if only because we have to.

David Puttnam

Extract reprinted with author's permission from pp 64-76 of The Third Age of Broadcasting, Ed Brian Wenham, Faber & Faber 1982

PINEWOOD STUDIOS

ACTUALLY WE'RE 47 YEARS OLD

years were all the rage. One's still struggling career ran the risk of falling between two stools.

But, though professionally precarious, it was a heady period. Experiment was in the air - in technique, in story telling, in theme and subject matter. Long established technical and artistic 'rules' were questioned and many of them went out of the window. Cinema was suddenly young again, and different and exciting. It was the period of Luc Goddard and Fellini, of *Un Bout du Souffle* and *8½*. To pick one's way through this period could be professionally schizophrenic.

In the early sixties I made two utterly different kinds of picture practically back to back - *Cairo* for MGM (in Cairo, to utilise the company's frozen funds there) which was a traditional, not to say old-fashioned, *genre* thriller, - in fact, it was a thinly disguised remake of John Huston's classic *The Asphalt Jungle,* relocated from California to Egypt; and *The World Ten Times Over,* a story of my own, made for my own company in co-production with ABPC which, in subject matter and treatment, was very much a sixties type 'new' movie.

An important influence upon the new way of making movies was the rise of the television commercial. In the early days it was mainly feature film directors who were called in to handle these 30-second mini movies. At a time when we had to adjust economically to a contractless world, going from picture to picture as it were, they provided a useful financial buffer between feature film assignments. But they also taught us to re-explore the medium, to use the most effective means of putting across the message in the screentime available, to be diamond sharp and precise to the second, to make every frame count. Much of what was learnt from this spilt over into the new styles of feature films.

But in spite of all this aesthetic revolutionary excitement, the commercial decline of the British cinema marched

relentlessly on. By the end of the decade, the brief bonanza of Swinging London was over. The Americans, who had been the main investors in the new British Film, withdrew their support and retired back to California. And the director, struggling to survive both professionally and financially, found himself forced to become another kind of creature - not only a director but an initiator of his own projects, a raiser of finances, a hustler and a self-promoter. With so many projects (and directors) chasing so little available finance, one found 90 per cent of one's time and energy spent in trying to get a picture set up, and only 10 per cent actually making it. *If* you were lucky! - for frustration became the order of the day when you might spend years pursuing a particular project and never get it off the ground.

And so we enter the lean seventies, the transitional period when feature film production in England was virtually confined to the Bond pictures, a spate of soft-porn tit and bum movies, and a few, very few and becoming annually fewer, serious indigenous productions. The fact was that, without subsidies, Britain could no longer support serious commercial native film production because no film could hope to get its money back from the ever diminishing British theatres alone.

Meanwhile, in America, there was a brief surge of epic multi-million-dollar productions and a series of so-called disaster movies to wean audiences away from their home screens. Some of these were made in British studios with British technicians because they were acknowledged to be the best in the world; but of course they rarely provided work for British directors, and we were slowly becoming an almost exclusively service industry.

Apart therefore from a handful of directors who had established international reputations and/or - like Peter Yates and John Boorman - found success and a professional base in Hollywood, we had a thin time of it. In my first year as director I made five, albeit low-budget, features. In the following ten years I averaged a film every 18 months or so. Between 1970 and 1980 I made precisely two films. Even directors more widely renowned, like Lindsay Anderson or Dick Lester, were sometimes three or four years between pictures.

At the same time, television commercials which provided the bulk of the work for film technicians relied less and less on feature directors, for they had begun to develop their own directorial talent who worked exclusively on commercials. It was from the ranks of these that, towards the end of the seventies, a new breed of feature director emerged - the Alan Parkers and Ridley Scotts and Hugh Hudsons. They had an enormous influence

The Conkordat

Three Hungarian brothers who arrived in Britain in the early 1930s had an enormous impact, and some would say not always a happy one, upon the development of the British film industry. Never steal two chickens from the same village goes a Hungarian gypsy proverb, but for the Kordas, or the eldest brother, Alexander, the underdeveloped British film industry was a village from which a single chicken had yet to be stolen!

Of the three Kordas, Vincent, the youngest brother who worked as an art director, was the most sympathetic to the film unions. Whereas Zoltan (who spent most of his later career as a director in America) was impatient and Alex was distant, Vincent felt more at home among carpenters, plasterers, gaffers and technicians, and he regarded them with a genuine (if slightly patronising) affection and respect as 'his boys'. He once outraged a visiting American producer by telling him that the studio carpenters put in a harder day's work than he did and he preferred people who, like himself, did not mind getting their hands dirty in the interests of art and craftmanship. His son, Michael Korda, who wrote the brilliant biography of his family, *Charmed Lives,* remembers his father telling him, 'The people who do the work are more important than the people who give the orders, and don't ever forget'.

Not surprisingly, the autocratic Sir Alex Korda, delegated the amiable Vincent to run his studio and liaise with the shop stewards. Alex wanted to continue working in his old way - starting late in the morning and finishing late at night if necessary - and he deeply resently the existence of an authority that paralleled his own at the studio. Apparently, Vincent managed to use his mediator's role to good effect when Alex was trying to persuade him to travel to work in a Rolls Royce, as befitted a Korda. Vincent was able to continue using his Hillman Minx (albeit a chauffeur-driven one) for a time on the grounds that his bargaining relationship with the unions might be undermined if he arrived every day in a Rolls.

Vincent Korda actually joined ACT and he was so keen to keep himself in good standing that on one occasion, George Elvin recalls, he paid his current normal subscription three times within a fortnight.

Margaret Mulvihill

CONGRATULATIONS AND GOOD WISHES TO ACTT ON ITS 50th ANNIVERSARY

THORN EMI ELSTREE STUDIOS
"Our future is your success"

over developments in the early eighties - not least because the pictures they made managed to break through what might be called the 'Atlantic Barrier'.

In fact it was television - erstwhile the arch-enemy of the movie industry - which generally gave the profession a shot in the arm - by providing not only new television-reared talent, but also an increasing diversity of outlets. This, in turn, stimulated new production. On the one hand are the many slick, professional and highly popular filmed series. On the other there is a new kind of hand-made product, by fresh talent and on moderate budgets, which not only finds an outlet on the home screen but also in cinemas and which, cross-fertilised between the film and television industries, even shows, wonder of wonders! - a return for the money invested.

Finally, there is the new world of co-productions. Because the individual cost of making movies - even on modest budgets - has escalated to the point where it is difficult to find a single financing source, the load is often spread across more than one country. Film is, after all, an international language, and the co-production treaties, which the ACTT has latterly spent considerable efforts in negotiating, have resulted in yet another means of encouraging new films. There is, indeed, a stirring in the undergrowth.

Today's film director is a very different creature from the director of the fifties, and he functions in a far more complex world. When I began, 30 years ago, the job was simply to direct pictures, no more, no less, either under contract to a studio or as a freelance on assignments. If you had a subject of your own, you tried to place it with the studio for which you were working, or find a producer to set it up for you. You were exclusively concerned with actually making pictures.

Now you are a multi-media person and work for a variety of different outlets - today on a feature, tomorrow for television, next week on documentaries, and in between on commercials. And for weeks and weeks - sometimes for months - you're not working on anything except on generating work for yourself. This has become the major target for your energies. You will almost certainly not be under any long-term contract - and those telephone calls bringing you assignments are few and far between.

So you will always have a number of projects in various stages of development which, alone or in partnership with a producer, you are trying to get off the ground. For this you need special talents. You will have to find the money, out of your own or other people's pockets, to develop your projects to the point where you can attract production finance. You are part of a 'package' and very often have to play an active part in the packaging

process. You have to know not only about lenses and film grammar and story values and how to get performances from your actors; you also have to know about production finance and the intricacy of studio politics and where to go to place your project and how to play the film finance market. And, above all, how to make sure that you remain 'bankable'.

Above Charles and Oona Chaplin with the ACTT Honorary Membership scroll the director received in 1957.

You also have to know about electronic as well as film techniques. The technical processes and what can be achieved by their proper use have become so much more complex that you've got to be a bit of a boffin. To make certain kinds of pictures, you almost need to become a computer expert.

So - film maker, businessman, self-promoter, boffin, public relations expert. A daunting job and a daunting prospect. The simplicity has gone. You could get lost in the ramifications and forget that what it's about is telling stories through a mixture of sound and images, the best way you know how. You could spend months - years! - trying to get a favourite project set up and then find out you're flogging a dead horse. It's easy to get discouraged and think there must be an easier way to make a living.

On the other hand, these are exciting times - the possibilities, and the means of realising them, are more widely spread than ever. There are no taboos - you can make films about almost anything under the sun, if you can find somebody to back you. And there are more fascinating ways of making films, of telling your story, than ever before. And, anyway, when all is said and done, you're hooked. Once bitten by the bug, you've got it for life. And it certainly keeps you on your toes. No wonder that, as a species and in spite of the stress and uncertainties of their lives, film directors tend to reach a ripe old age, and often die in harness well past their alotted span of three score and ten.

Among my remaining ambitions, this one certainly figures high on the list.

ANGLIA TELEVISION
Producers of award-winning
drama and Survival wildlife
documentaries for the ITV Network
send warmest congratulations
on your
50th Anniversary

THE SECOND 'T'

Nineteen years after the birth of BBC Television came ITV. And the union found a powerful new role.

Commercial television is a closed shop. In other words, a person who is not a member of ACTT, or another appropriate union, may not be employed in jobs the scope of which is covered by agreements between the unions involved and the employers. This situation, which is in many respects analagous to the relations between members of liberal professions - doctors, lawyers, chartered accountants - and their professional associations, without whose approval they may not practise their trade, is a legacy of the early days of commercial television.

Until the 1950s, the BBC, a non-profit-making enterprise, was the only broadcasting institution in the country. Commercial television was instituted by a Conservative government, in response to pressure from a powerful political lobby whose members were interested in using television as a vehicle for profit-making.

Below First broadcast to schools. Sir Walford Davies with some of the Temple Church choirboys. **Right** The plaque at Alexandra Palace.

GREATER LONDON COUNCIL
THE WORLD'S FIRST REGULAR HIGH DEFINITION TELEVISION SERVICE WAS INAUGURATED HERE BY THE BBC 2 November 1936

Such entrepreneurs saw nothing threatening in a closed shop. On the contrary, the orderliness of recruitment, and the stability of employment that a closed shop implied, had an attraction for them. And despite the power it gave the unions, they have never made serious efforts to rewrite those agreements.

In April 1955 ACT made its debut in commercial television, with a strike for recognition as the official union of the technicians working in the new branch of the industry. Within a year the second "T"

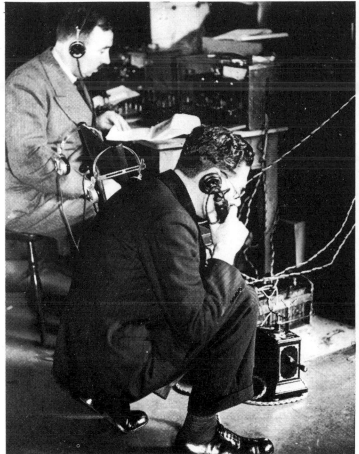

was added to the union's title, and for the first time just over a year later, in August 1957, the programme contractors put their signatures to the first agreement on behalf of the technicians employed in commercial television. By the end of the 1960s, ACTT had established itself as a major force within the television industry.

Throughout this time it had made its presence felt with the first and subsequent television agreements; negotiations over redundancy at Westward TV; the first national television strike in 1964; redeployment negotiations on behalf of its members following the reshuffling of the ITV contracts; a campaign for recognition at the BBC (where there had always been members), and the first of a series of talks, which are still going on today, about the possibility of a merger with the Association of Broadcasting Staff.

The great ITV lock-out

The longest - and most dramatic - industrial battle in the union's history took place between August and October 1979 when a ten-week lock-out blanked ITV screens.

ACTT had an impeccable case for a much better deal than the 16 per cent the companies originally offered. Figures were produced showing that, since 1975, members' pay had increased 46 per cent and ITV company profits had increased 189 per cent. On the union side, negotiations were conducted by TV Organiser Jack O'Connor, General Secretary Alan Sapper, and the TV

Branch negotiating committee. While talking went on behind closed doors, union members mounted an impressive information and publicity campaign to back up the negotiators' case.

Left Fallen giant. The 1,265ft ITA mast lies in the snow at Emley Moor in the Yorkshire Pennines, March 1969. For four days the fledgling Yorkshire Television was off the air while engineers worked against the clock in appalling conditions to erect a temporary 217ft mast brought by sea from Sweden. for those four days YTV's future looked bleak.

Right Doris Rogers fronted one of ITV's first advertising magazines, *What's in Store*, in 1956. **Far Right** Camera rehearsal at ABC studios. **Centre** Sound boom and operator at ABC Teddington studios, 1961.

Simon Albury, producer/director at Granada TV in London (he was then on *World in Action*) has vivid memories of those heady days. It was he and Jerry Kuehl who more or less appointed themselves to run the propaganda powerhouse in the Asquith Room at Number 2 Soho Square. Simon had recently picked up some useful tricks of the trade from an examination he had made of the operations of Winner and Wagner, 'professional political attitude changers' in California.

Over the ten weeks of the lock-out, Simon and Jerry - in collaboration with the union's headquarters staff and the help of some 40 members from the London ITV companies - conducted their impressive media campaign. They composed and sent out a dozen bulletins to the TV members, explaining the details of all offers and counter-proposals and

Below Alan Sapper pours the champagne for Thames TV (Euston) shop steward Peter Bould and (right) ACTT organiser Bob Hamilton after the important Hadmor legal victory of February 1982. **Right** Lord Denning.

preparing them for the next stage of the struggle. 'Early on, we got a letter from a member saying, "I now know how to argue with my friends in the local pub",' Simon recalls. 'That was important - the members were able to understand and explain why we deserved the money.'

Deserve the money, they did. And the long drawn out dispute ended pretty satisfactorily for the union. *Film and TV Technician* reported in the November 1979 issue, 'At the end of the

unprecedented ten-week dispute which completely closed down ITV's national network, members in ITV voted overwhelmingly to return to work on the basis of a formula covering pay, holidays and new technology.' The pay package was estimated by the TV negotiating committee to be worth between 44 and 45 per cent by July 1980.

An unforgettable memory

Never get into litigation if you don't have to. That is one of the good rules followed by sensible people and by sensible trade unions. Other people don't follow the rule and many of them have pursued the union through the courts over the years. The most celebrated case involving ACTT was the Hadmor case, brought against union officers and officials in 1981. It was the first case to be brought to the House of Lords under the 1980 Employment Act and the union won a major legal victory before their Lordships on 11 February 1982.

Lord Diplock and four other Law Lords then granted an appeal from the union, whose officers and members had been taken to court for threatening industrial action at Thames Television because of an anticipated loss of jobs. The Law Lords reversed a Court of Appeal judgment delivered in April 1981 when the then Master of the Rolls, the controversial Lord Denning, had granted an injunction to Hadmor Productions Ltd, whose TV series *Unforgettable* had been blacked by the union's television branch.

Union members had feared for their jobs when a product was bought in cheaply from a facility company at a time when their own studios were underemployed. Hadmor had argued that the issue at Thames TV in February 1981 was not a legitimate industrial dispute, and that those threatening or taking industrial action were unlawfully interfering with business. Lord Diplock said – and his fellow Law Lords agreed – that fear of redundancy could be a legitimate cause of an industrial dispute.

Incidentally, Lord Diplock (whose judgment restored the decision of Mr Justice Dillon in February 1981 not to grant an injunction to Hadmor) had some severe things to say about Lord Denning. He criticised the Master of the Rolls for breaking a long established convention which disallows quotation from Hansard in support of legal argument. Lord Denning did quote Hansard and Lord Diplock observed, "For a judge to disregard the rule by which counsel are bound has the effect of depriving the parties to the action of the benefit of one of the most fundamental rules of natural justice". It had been argued by Hadmor's counsel that one of the effects of the 1980 Employment Act was to remove immunity from trade unionists in this situation, but this was described by Lord Diplock as 'not giving the words of the statute their plain and unambiguous meaning'.

While the Law Lords found in favour of the union, Hadmor did not withdraw their claim for damages against ACTT and its officers and members for a sum in excess of £1 million. It has not been pursued since.

ACTT General Secretary, Alan Sapper, commented on the Lords' historic decision. 'The courts rarely find in favour of the truth where trade unionists are concerned, and this has been a great exception. This case, to a limited extent, weakens the attacks by the present government on the trade union movement. And it tames a reactionary Court of Appeal.' The Hadmor case, which earned its place in the law books and journals, at the same time immortalised the name of ACTT National Organiser, Bob Hamilton – lawyers of the future will always refer to the case of Hadmor Productions Ltd and Others v Hamilton and Others.

Peter Avis

Note: Parts of The Unforgettable series were later shown on Channel 4, without further dispute or litigation.

Television never stops still, either in its scope or its technology. The frontiers have been dramtically extended since the lock-out of 1979 and — with cable and satellite on the horizon — we have already absorbed a second ITV service, Channel 4, and the habit-changing advent of breakfast television.

When Channel 4 went on screen on 2 November 1982, it did so with the warm support of ACTT. The union's shop steward there, Cherry Coles, said, "We are conscious that we have a great responsibility to the industry as a whole. What Channel 4 will do is to open up a whole new spectrum of work. It will lead to more people being employed. And it will give them more scope for creativity".

In the long debates about what sort of service the new channel would provide, ACTT had stood firmly against proposals that it should be merely ITV2, a carbon copy of what already existed. The union had welcomed a channel that would enable both independent film-makers and those permanently employed in independent television to present their work to a new audience.

When, after the launching of Channel 4, the service came under attack from those who were offended by its enlightened and innovatory approach, General Secretary Alan Sapper declared, "We don't believe that it is in the country's or the industry's interest that Channel 4 should be destroyed by the barbarians".

In the 1980s, the whole question of how ITV franchises are allocated and reallocated — and how ITV workers' lives are ordered and disordered — has become an important issue for ACTT, for other broadcasting unions and for the whole trade union movement.

Dennis Sippings, then ACTT Vice-President, put it sharply at the 1982 Trades Union Congress at Brighton, when he denounced the 'cynical manner in which lives are ordered and disrupted, and jobs are endangered'.

He was proposing a composite resolution, which delegates passed unanimously, deploring the fact that 'the powers given to the IBA periodically to award independent television franchises take so little account of trade union interests within the broadcasting industry.

'The situation of studio closures and enforced moving of homes to protect jobs and pension rights, where indeed this is possible, cannot be tolerated', said the resolution. 'The extensive uncertainty and disruption caused to the working and personal lives of many men and women, in particular at the former ATV (now Central) studios at Elstree, challenge the IBA's justification of its powers as being in the interests of the public and the consumer.

'Conscious of the turmoil in which people who work in ITV have been placed yet again by the decision of the IBA in relation to franchise reallocations, Congress demands that the IBA be obliged by statute to secure a commitment from prospective contractors, whether for independent television or local radio, to give full protection to the working conditions and pension arrangements of any union members concerned.

'Congress calls for greater accountability of the IBA and for greater trade union consultation over the long-term planning of the broadcasting industry, as a means of regulating the broadcasting industry, which takes equal account of the public interest and that of the workers who maintain the industry'.

The unanimous resolution from the 1982 TUC — proposed by ACTT — summed up well the position of the union as it faced the challenges of the third age of broadcasting.

50 years on– and the latest on the changing face of ITV...

CENTRAL

getting to the heart of the Midlands

CENTRAL INDEPENDENT TELEVISION plc.

BIRMINGHAM Central House, Broad Street, Birmingham B1 2JP. Telephone: 021-643 9898 (Telex 338966)
OXFORD Albion House, 1 Albion Place, Oxford OX1 1SL. Telephone: 0865-725358/9
NOTTINGHAM Newland House, Mount Street, Nottingham NG1 6GN. Telephone: 0602-413111 (Telex 377696)
LEICESTER 6th Floor, Epic House, Charles Street, Leicester LE1 3SH. Telephone: 0533-538915

INTELLIGENT LIFE
NORTH OF
WATFORD

T*he union was dragged screaming into the age of commercial television. Kurt Lewenhak, who was there at the birth, tells his own story of how ACT acquired a second 'T'.*

I'm not too keen on celebrating institutional anniversaries as a rule. They often lend themselves to the pronouncement of complacent obituaries over still warm bodies. But perhaps the fact that in 1955, our union entered the lists and started to organise in commercial television should not be allowed to pass wholly unremarked. (For not only did it add the second 'T' to our initials, but it involved the discovery of intelligent life north of Watford by those to the south of that border town).

Below The signing of the first ACTT/Programme Contractors' Association National Agreement in 1957. Present were George Elvin, Alf Cooper, Ken Roberts, Paddy Leech, Captain Brownrigg (Rediffusion TV) Lew Grade (ATV), Tony Shine (RTV Shop steward).

It is difficult to recall now, but Annual General Meetings in the far-off days of the Association of Cine-Technicians were less formal trade union functions than boisterous tribal gatherings, with the suede shoes, camel-hair coats and battered Bentleys of the Features Branch fraternising, or not, with the leather-patched elbows of Documentary and only

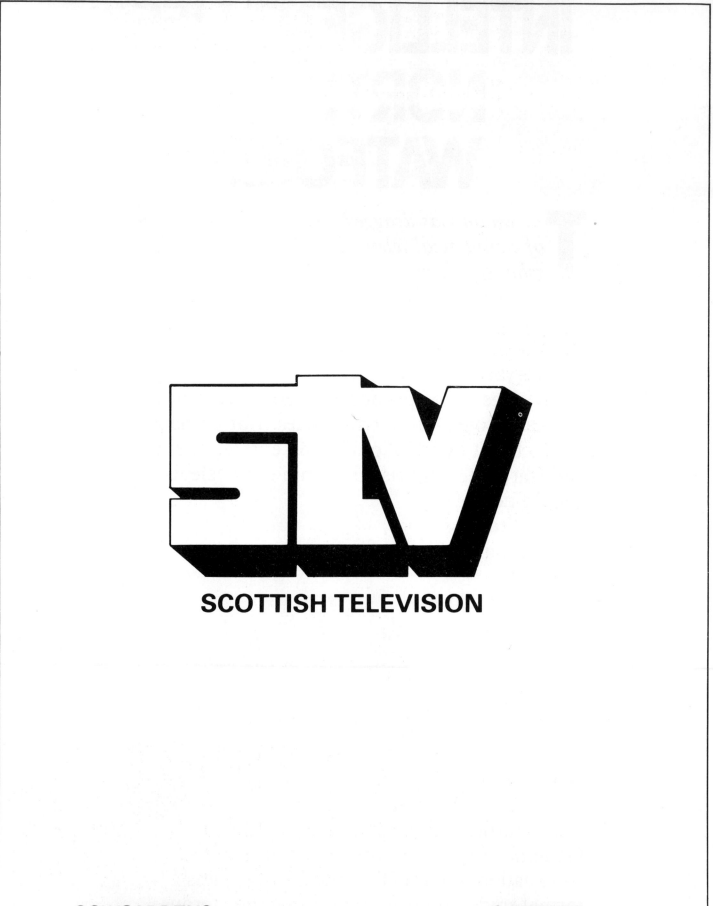

SCOTTISH TELEVISION

**COWCADDENS·
GLASGOW**

**GATEWAY·
EDINBURGH**

the Labs in respectable three-piece suits. Despite these marginal differences in style, the tribe was a small friendly one occupying its traditional hunting grounds in west and north-west London. We all spoke the same language, more or less.

Imagine then, the consternation at one of these well-ordered ritual reunions (held in 1956 for some reason on Hudson Bay fur-trapper territory in the Beaver Hall in the City) when the first ever provincial television delegation from Manchester trooped in. I probably affected a cloth cap; gangling Michael Scott wore a muffler; all that we lacked to complete the metropolitan stereotype of a northern outing was a football rattle! History of a sort was being made. The cosy Annual General Meeting - all members in good standing welcome - had been transformed into a National Delegate Conference and the union had earned its double 'T'.

How had it all come about? Before the advent of ITV, as it came to be called, the union had resolutely opposed the introduction of commercial television. Nevertheless, with admirable pragmatism, once the first London television companies began transmission, union members working within them began to set up shops. There was even an early stoppage at Rediffusion's Wembley Studios, which provoked the now legendary response of 'Mutiny by God' from the quarter-deck-oriented management. (I'll swear that even years later a Rediffusion personnel officer visiting one of their OB crews, with whom I was working at the London Zoo, explained that he had 'just come along to see that everything was ship-shape and Bristol fashion, and in accordance with our treaty with ACTT squared!'. Naval tradition is nothing if not resilient). At the same time as ACT members were serving their time before the mast at Wembley, other union stalwarts such as Vic Rudolf were bringing the light to outer London Moss Empires in Wood Green and Hackney, working for ATV.

A little later, in the backroom of a rather sad Manchester pub, The Balking Donkey, three newly-appointed employees of the embryonic Granada Television Service found that they had union membership in common. They were Sally Mathews, Jack Bartlett and me. We decided to book a room in a slightly more cheerful pub and to invite ACT to send up an organiser to address us and our fellows. Enthusiasm for a shop was not too great. Some of my fellow trainee directors hailed from repertory theatre where £20 a week with no weeks 'out' seemed a haven of snug security. But setting up our shop and achieving company recognition were only the first steps - a far longer struggle ensued to achieve adequate representation in the affairs of the union.

ACT had always prided itself on its democratic structure and accessibility - all shops had, as they still have, the right to be represented on the General Council. All members had, as they still have, the right to attend Annual Conference. This worked well while the membership was concentrated in the Greater London area, but once we started to have a provincial membership - the Granada shop in Manchester was soon followed by others in the ITV capitals - the position altered dramatically. It was true that in 'film only' days a few brave spirits had tried to make documentaries for the Co-op and other organisations in Manchester. A studio with fluctuating fortunes had even functioned intermittently in that city, producing films starring northern music-hall comics. But in organisational and cultural terms, the film industry had been centred on the metropolis. And even if we had been able to organise effectively in the BBC, which for a host of reasons we were not, BBC television barely extended beyond the capital and the Home Counties.

But with the coming of Granada and other ITV companies, permanent settlements of TV and film technicians were putting down roots in the main provincial centres. It was no use telling those members that they enjoyed equal rights with the London members to drift, more or less at will, into Number 2 Soho Square. The whole costly business of

Above Granada technicians getting ready to televise a debate at the Rochdale by-election in February 1958. **Below** Granada OB crew being sworn in by the Returning Officer to give them access to the counting of the votes at the by-election.

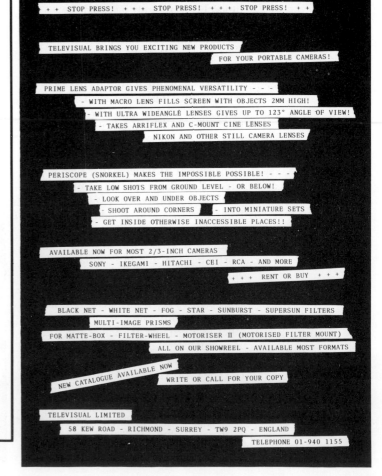
112

paying fares and overnight allowances so that provincial delegates could attend TV Branch, General Council and Annual Conference meetings had to be tackled before the TV members became fully enfranchised.

In making a nationwide rather than a local union, in encompassing a new mass medium of tremendous potency and pervasiveness, the nature of the original ACT obviously changed. But the union's fundamental characteristics as a friendly, democratic and progressive organisation did not, in my view, alter. Initially, there certainly were tensions between the old and new memberships. The Film Camera Section took time to learn that a demand for a stringer cameraman in West Hartlepool or Penzance was not the same as a vacancy in Wardour Street. Per contra, the new member stringer cameraman in the provinces had to be restrained by rule from rushing down to London to compete for the few camera jobs available. Nevertheless, the new members on the TV Branch Committee soon learned the ropes, with the help in some cases of old film-hands like Ivor Montagu, whom they appointed as their advisor.

So, what lessons are to be learned from the union's entry into, and experience of, ITV? First, was the union right to oppose commercial television — or were its fears misplaced? It is almost impossible to assess the political, social and economic effects of commercial television on its own, for the inter-relationships between the media and our mass consumer society are complex. All one can do, short of a massive research project, is to hazard one's own guesses. On the whole, the interruptions of 'commercials' have not bowdlerised and cheapened programmes as much as was once feared, though the editorial pressure of the advertisers is none the less real for being discreetly applied. When did you last see a programme fundamentally critical of, say, the oil industry on ITV?

On the other hand, particularly in the growth period when the ITV companies were still trying to build up their audiences, or now when they are trying to impress a public enquiry, ITV programme-makers are permitted to tackle controversial public issues. Certainly, it was ITV that initially broke through many of the middle-class taboos with which the BBC had dutifully shielded the establishment. In the rivalry for mass audiences some areas of public debate have been extended. In the early days of CND, for example, while ACTT members made the film of the Aldermaston March, and the BBC banned *The War Game*, Granada was persuaded to commission J B Priestley to write *Doomsday for Dyson*. Even if the ITA, as it then was, did demand that it be followed by a 'balanced

Above Early Aldermaston marchers.

discussion', the play was transmitted.

ITV put the provinces on the map and for the first time, in television drama, working-class people were portrayed in leading roles, rather than merely as supporting players. But, according to some media sociologists, it is not the programmes that carry the channel's main message, but the commercials. Only in this sense is Marshall McLuhan's dictum about the medium being the message true. However much our sensibilities have been affected, our consciences pricked, by some 20-odd minutes of uninterrupted programme content, the commercial break reassures us. In the self-centred, high-gloss world of instant gratification, all is for the best - spending is action, and possessions, particularly consumer durables, lead to security, fulfilment and happiness. Who can say how much of a part this constant 'drip' plays in conditioning people into accepting values they might otherwise reject? At least, one can understand why our union forebears were profoundly sceptical about the promised benefits of commercial television.

On the industrial level, we have clearly gained from the recruitment of a large number of highly-skilled and, on the whole, highly-paid members, who have given us an insider's place in the electronic revolution that is changing the communication pattern of our industry. If we had tried before ITV to restructure the union to suit an expected influx of television members, it is doubtful whether we would have arrived at our present arrangements or anything better. Instead we reacted, not always quickly enough and sometimes even grudgingly, to our perception of the changing needs of our members and to the pressure generated by them. The response may not have been elegant in constitutional terms, but it enabled us to accomplish a sea-change without foundering. It is to be hoped that in the future our union will continue to be responsive to the needs of the members and as flexible in facing changes in the industries in which we operate, while at the same time continuing to adhere to the principles that made ACT/ACTT worth belonging to, both before and after the coming of ITV.

INDEPENDENT TELEVISION SERVING THE SOUTH AND SOUTH-EAST

NATURAL BREAK

John Fletcher — who has made some distinguished ones — looks at commercials and the changing manners they portray.

Twenty-five years ago I stood in Switzerland overlooking the village of St Cergue waiting, with frozen feet, for what I do not remember, some particular quality of the light perhaps, or the motor on an enormous snowplough to be fixed, or something of that ilk. I was there on behalf of a British production house, directing a commercial for an American agency that was advertising a German motor car, Volkswagen. I and my colleagues did not know it but we were actually there making history, since after winning the first prize at the Venice advertising film festival for that year, that piece of celluloid was placed in the Museum of Modern Art in New York

Left John Fletcher plus museum piece — a Vinten|H.

as one of the ten best commercials ever made, perhaps even now it lies in a time capsule on the moon. Ars Brevis Vita Longis. Would that all my work achieved such a distinguished resting place!

The birth of the TV commercial

In 1955 ITV was born and with it the TV advertising commercial. It was treated with disdain by the established film professionals. No one really knew how to capture an audience's attention in 30 seconds, or indeed wanted to know. After all, real cinema was busy with drama. Impact was regarded as cheap effect. Directors tended to resent spending time directing a bottle of Wincarnis, or a handful of coffee beans. And anyway, how many different faces can an actor pull to express delight and pleasure? Bazazz made craftsmanship cringe.

Can you remember the world of those times, with basic middle-class reserve and Home Counties values. The fading days of Uncle Mac by Vicky - the lion's tail being tweaked in an Egyptian mincer while Hungary's freedom bled to death. Nothing much had changed since that war ended 15 years earlier. A few cockney millionaires had emerged. George Dawson had made a fortune selling the army it's own lorries. The middle classes continued to bemoan the working class's loss of innocence, while the film industry continued to make a crisis out of a drama.

Above You're never alone with a Strand.

Now it is a sad frailty of human nature that anything new that threatens to tilt the applecart is resented by most ordinary folk. It's probably some primeval defensive reflex at work. A highly developed sense that enabled our cave-dwelling ancestors to get a good night's sleep when surrounded by yowling carnivores. However derived, this human reflex persists as an innate suspicion of anything innovative or new.

The zest of the 1960s

Then we hit the 1960s, and suddenly things began to move. Starting in art and design, a whole new culture of youth and

vitality changed the tone of society. It was down to a new generation who wanted to succeed on their own terms and by their own standards. Photographers who would explore and popularise new images in graphic art. Musicians who would re-establish the skill of the ballad in popular and contemporary social terms, and who would find their own audience, their own generation internationally. Hard workers, they showed that it was possible to be young, internationally successful and a millionaire before 30. Zest was in the air!

It even reached to the very top of society. The Prime Minister was photographed in a Beatles' wig. And a princess of the realm married a commoner - an old Etonian photographer - who designed expensive birdcages in his spare time.

Values converged and the disciplines of advertising changed as a new generation of visual artists rediscovered that making a product look good was what Hollywood was about. Suddenly those 30-second slots were no longer about sausages or booze - they were about feelings, and getting through to the audience's sense of self-esteem. Agency directors began to talk less about the product and more about the sense of pleasure and freedom to be had by owning, using or identifying with the product.

Sensation became the accompaniment, youth the theme. There was a hubble bubble of ideas as new directors fought to create their own kind of world, and to generate their own value images.

Fairy snow became gentle.

The Alfa Romeo became sexy.

Rolex watches became distinguished.

And any mother who cared, next to her family, preferred Tide - Clean Clothes!

Meanwhile, in the USA, the question was posed of the then President, 'Would you buy a used car from this man?'.

Commercials during the 1960s rose to be one of the largest consistent employers of film production resources. With a declining national production they and television documentaries more than sustained the industry in volume of work, and more and more people were drawn into the production scene. Since pro-rata the cost per minute of final screen time was ten times greater than fictional film, manufacturers began to produce specialist equipment to fulfil the imaginative demands of the new graphic medium.

Out of television documentary practice too, came many exciting devices - new lightweight lighting equipment, Lowell lights and gaffer tape, Sunguns and Colortran. To examine the pack more closely the Macro Kilar lens stepped in and the zoom lens was adapted and pressed into service. I remember an early bolt-on gyroscope derived from a gunsight. It weighed a ton, howled like a banshee and needed a separate crew member who risked a hernia carrying (usually running with) the battery.

In praise of the commercial

What have commercials done for the current industry? Most of our great contemporary cineastes - people like Alan Parker or David Puttnam - emerged from the halcyon days of the 1960s commercial. They represent a generation that learned to entertain by first learning how to capture an audience's attention. The money that flowed into the industry created new and innovative equipment, which has now become a part of the toolkit of any film-maker.

'How do you get to Carnegie Hall?'

'Practice!'

Where else could the young film-maker get to experiment with so much freedom, or the young camera person try out a novel idea. Sure it might not work, but in the experiment exciting ways of conveying information could emerge. Britain became renowned for all its technical and imaginative skills in the field of motion picture production, through an obvious expertise and experience in advertising commercials. Every commercial shown overseas became a banner for British skills and talent.

And what of the world twenty-five years on? Who could have conceived that Auntie BBC would be running a disc jockey show, or *Top of the Pops*? That a cabinet minister might find himself publicly answerable for his decisions to a cross section of the public assembled in the studio? That on the box one could find advice to teenagers on VD or training in higher maths for a degree, or personal counselling on family problems? More people are more informed on more topics via television than was conceivable in the 1950s.

Perhaps it's because of this fact that the posture of government has gone full circle and firm decisiveness has again become the order of the day. Anthony Eden and Margaret Thatcher have something in common. We may have contributed to television and the TV commercial, but TV has and will continue to change our entire perception of the world.

Left Manhattan coming into land - British Airways, 1983.

Broadcast..

...STILL

the broadcasting industry's weekly newspaper

DANGLERS
AND DROP-LINES

David Edgar is one of 500 screenwriters who *are members of ACTT. 'Writers have the suspicion that nobody else believes they have a craft', he says. And that is only one of their problems as they cope with censors and other philistines.*

I suppose every screenwriter's done it at one time or another. It's when (for the 20th time) your nervous and tentative suggestions about how your work should be shot have been blinded by science, ("Yes, David, fine, but number three would fall over the boom." "Yes, David, great, that's what we call in the trade a jump-shot."), and you kneel to the writers' saint (St Francis de Sales, according to Brewer) and pray, 'Please, dear St Francis, give me some jargon'. In my case, the subsequent dialogue went like this.

Above David Edgar speaking at an ACTT Annual Conference. **Left** Shooting his adaptation of *Nicholas Nickleby*.

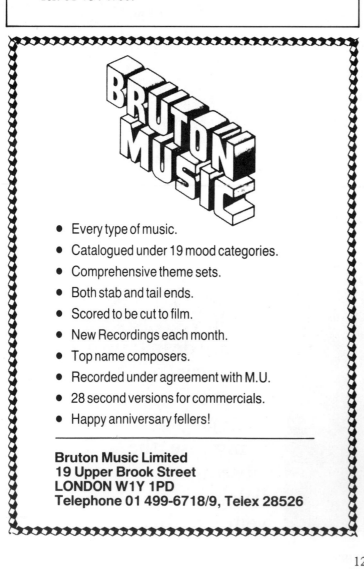

DIRECTOR: Look, David, I think the scene's magic. There's just this problem with the last line. Do you see what I mean?

ME: (AFTER A SIGNIFICANT PAUSE) Yuh, well, Adrian.... I think the basic problem we have here is that I've written a suspended drop-line and it should be a dangler.

(ANOTHER PAUSE)

DIRECTOR: Beg pardon? (YET ANOTHER PAUSE) Oh, a dangler. Yes. Of course. As opposed to.... the other thing you said. Yes, well. No problem. Shove in a - ?

ME: Dangler.

DIRECTOR: Dangler, and we'll be right as rain.

Now, of course, while danglers certainly exist (there's one in the above dialogue), writers don't always call them that, any more than suspended drop-lines (there's one of them too) are necessarily called that by anyone except me. The point is that writers have the suspicion that nobody else really believes they have a craft. After all, not everybody can play the violin, or indeed work a camera or edit film, but everybody can and does write things down, and (as any script editor will tell you) the writing of dramatic fiction is more or less a national hobby. Some writers - it will be acknowledged - are better at their hobby than others; but hobby it remains, and the process of the creation of film or television drama is seen (we suspect, in our paranoid way) as the realisation, by a group of hard-nosed professionals, of the inspired but often incoherent vision of gifted amateurs.

There are two main reasons for this state of affairs. One is that writers do the bulk of their work before most of the other professionals are even engaged; and even if they are re-writing like billy-o throughout the rehearsal and recording periods, they tend even then to do their thing alone. One of the many good things about writers being involved in a technicians' union is that it allows other professionals to meet writers (and vice versa), and to gather a little of their problems and concerns, in formal meetings, in the pub afterwards, and indeed, as now, in print.

At the moment, there are a large number of such problems and concerns. The first is the defence of that jewel in the crown of British dramatic broadcasting, the single, one-off television play. Ever since this creature declined into extinction in the United States, we have known that it exists on sufferance here. The form -

expensive, dangerous, controversial - it is important not just because it has produced dozens and dozens of really great programmes (from *Cathy Come Home* to the work of Dennis Potter); it is also important because the discoveries made in the single play inform and deepen the way that series and serials are made. One obvious, symbolic example is the series

Boys from the Blackstuff, which grew out of a single Play for Today; but in my view it is also undeniable that series and serials as various as *Minder, Brideshead Revisited* and *Bill Brand* owed much of their sophistication and quality to developments in the art that occurred first in the single play. This form is thus the grit in the oyster - while *Play for Today* is still with us, we will not descend into the bland morass of American formula programming.

Above Carol White as Cathy in Jeremy Sandford's epoch-forming television play *Cathy Come Home,* BBC 1966. **Below** *Boys from the Blackstuff.*

The second major problem television writers face is censorship. The screenwriter and director David Hare (director/author of *Licking Hitler* and *Dreams of Leaving*) recently argued in a book of articles by screenwriters[1] that the reason why the BBC hierarchy (in particular) didn't understand how bothered writers get about censorship is because the top level of that hierarchy consists largely of journalists, used to getting their work rewritten by others, or even spiked. The reason why dramatic writers feel so strongly that their work should not be treated in this way is because they are aware that no dictatorship - even if it has allowed freedom of worship, or freedom for the non-literary arts - has ever left writers alone. It is no coincidence that Mary Whitehouse has been consistently concerned not just with 'bad language' and nudity but also with programmes whose political content she found displeasing (from *Cathy Come Home* onwards). As Trevor Griffiths pointed out in 1980[2], there has been consistent censorship, covert and overt, external and self-imposed, of plays about Northern Ireland. Roy Minton's *Scum* was not banned because of its violence, but because it mounted a wholesale attack on an important political institution, the penal system for young offenders.

In the last couple of years, a whole new pressure for censorship has been allowed to emerge, in the form of the Broadcasting Complaints Commission, set up under the government's Broadcasting Act, which poses a severe threat to one of the most important dramatic forms to be created by television, the drama-documentary[3]. ACTT writers were particularly pleased that the union's motion to the 1981 TUC dealt with the BCC, and hope that the union will continue its efforts to monitor the workings of this dubious institution, and to work for its disbandment, or at least reform.

A third concern, shared by writers and all other broadcasters and film-makers, is with the new technology (with its perhaps suitable acronym 'TNT'). The residual structure for writers - often vital for a writer to earn from his or her work a sum commensurate with the time it took to write - is under severe threat from the uncontrollable and unpoliceable expansion of cable, satellite and video outlets. Writers, as the owners of the copyright in their work (on television if not, sadly, in film) are in a slightly different - and more difficult - position to other professionals who receive residuals. But clearly it is important that writers work together with other affected broadcasters and film-makers to find ways of living with and in the multi-outlet universe.

The final concern I'd like to mention is a rather more personal one. Like many new British screenwriters, (including Stephen Poliakoff, Alan Bleasedale and Trevor Griffiths) I started my career in the alternative theatre, and continue to move between the two media. One of the most exciting things to happen in the theatre over the last 20 years is the breaking-down of the traditional professional hierarchies, and the development of a much more fluid approach to the relationship between directors, actors, designers and writers. In particular, alternative and indeed now mainstream theatre have begun to find ways in which the processes of writing and production can be much more collaborative, while retaining the input of (and respect for) individual skills.

The barriers against collaborative work between writers, directors, performers and technicians are clearly much greater in television, where the complexity and expense of the technology (and the personnel!) militate for a rigid division of labour. But, in an era when live television drama is returning to our screens, and Channel 4 is mounting a brave assault on the traditional assumptions of programme-making, perhaps this is an appropriate moment to express the hope that some of the discoveries made in the theatre about new techniques of play-making could be applied to the electronic media.

As I've said, writers are often accused of being prey to paranoia about their relationship to the arts they service. We are sometimes justly accused of misunderstanding the importance of other creative roles. I work in collective media like theatre, television, radio and film because I find my work is best when it is mediated through the creativity of many other people. (If I didn't think that I'd write novels). Trade unions are not (and should not be) directly concerned with aesthetic matters. But by bringing together all kinds of professionals, engaged in a common endeavour, a union like ACTT inevitably aids and abets the creation of the kind of collaborative spirit which I've been trying to describe. Who knows? After my next meeting, someone might explain to me what a jump-shot actually is.

1 Ah! Mischief: The Writer and Television, Faber & Faber, 1982

2 Summarised in The Television Play and Contemporary Society, Goldsmiths' College, London, 1981

3 For further detail, see my article on drama documentary, in Ah! Mischief, ibid.

Right George Bernard Shaw, 'Irishman, vegetarian, social democrat, lecturer and debater, a fierce opponent of the present status of women and insister on the serious-ness of art', replied with typically devastating wit to a questionnaire from *The Cine-Technician* in 1939.

1: Did "Pygmalion" lose any of its force in being transferred to the screen ? *No.*

2. Do you think Hollywood could have made a better version of "Pygmalion" ? *No: Hollywood would have murdered Pygmalion. That is why Hollywood did not get it.*

3. Which film version of "Pygmalion" do you prefer - the earlier Dutch one, or the recent British one ? And why ? *I prefer my own version, which is substantially that followed by Mr Gabriel Pascal.*

4. It has been said that on the screen "Pygmalion" dates and seems old fashioned. What is your opinion ? *Anything that is not the latest ephemeral Californian slang seems old fashioned in that benighted State. I write English — and vernacular English.*

5. Are you likely to write directly for the screen ? If not, why not ? *My stuff is as good on the screen as on the stage.*

6. What is your opinion of screenwriting as a profession ? Is the scenario-writer necessary ? *That depends on how much the author leaves undone. The author, if a playwright, should do everything except the shooting script.*

7. Would you agree that it is essential for the well being of the British film industry that it should recognise the organisations representing its technicians, and make agreements with them ? *Of course it should.*

8. Have you seen any films which you think are the equal, from artistic or propagandist reasons, of your own work in the theatre ? *What do you mean by "equal"? Nothing, apparently. Pass on.*

9. Do you think the British Board of Film Censors is necessary ? *It is only a contrivance to enable timid film firms to give themselves certificates of decency.*

10. Do you think the British film industry has any future ? *Of course I do. Do you think London Bridge has any future ?*

11. Now that you have joined your professional organisation (The Screenwriters' Association), are you also going to join your appropriate Trade Union in the film industry - The Association of Cine-Technicians ? *I am not a cine-technician: I am a playwright.*

12. Who in your opinion is the second greatest dramatist in the world ? *I do not know; and neither do you. You must wait a few centuries for your answer.*

-------------oOo-----------

It has licensed some films that have driven me from the theatre by their dull lubricity, and simultaneously banned a film to which it ought to have given a gold medal for distinguished service to public morals. Such certificates are worthless and sometimes mischievous.

123

GUNPOWDER AND SMOKE

British special effects technicians — protected by tight safety regulations negotiated by the union — are world renowned. Cliff Richardson looks back on an exciting career.

Cliff Richardson, doyen of British special effects, began his long career in 1921, helping his brother who worked in a small Clapham film studio. That experience whetted his appetite for film, but when he left school he wanted to become a chemist. Instead, however, he found himself apprenticed to a small tool-making firm. Though he didn't finish his apprenticeship as an engineer, his experience in the workshop (and his initial aspirations as a chemist) were to be, literally, of good effect when he found his real metier as a maker of special effects for films.

In this capacity, he started at British International Pictures in Elstree in 1926, having been alerted to a job there by Chris Chapman, who had been the property-master at the old studio in Clapham.

Right Cliff Richardson connects a black burster for *Red Beret*. The joke was for the benefit of lighting man John Wilcox.

125

‘ The studios looked like airship sheds in the middle of a muddy field. I was introduced to the members of the property department, who were mostly from West End theatres, and I was given a personally conducted tour by Chris. Hitchcock was making *The Ring* with Lillian Hall-Davis, Carl Brisson, Ian Hunter and Gordon Harker, while on another stage Arthur Maude was shooting interiors for *Poppies of Flanders* starring Jameson Thomas, Eve Gray and Malcolm Todd. I was delegated to look after the battle effects on *Poppies of Flanders,* which only amounted to a few ground explosions representing shellfire.

I cannot remember the words ‘special effects’ being used, although during my six-year period at BIP, I met the very versatile Italian model-maker Guidobaldi, who was known affectionately throughout the studios as Guido. I also saw the development of tricks, or special processes as they were then called, the cut-out matt, glass matt, foreground or hanging miniatures, the Schufftan process, the Dunning process, etc. On Walter Summers’ film *Suspense* I was put in charge of the battle effects, which were on a fairly large scale.

Even today I shudder to think of the chances that were taken in making up charges of flash powder, especially at night when it only needed a wind-carried spark from a cigarette to set the whole lot off. Switchboards were another hazard, as they were usually of the bellpush type. We were extremely lucky to finish the film with only two minor casualties. I suffered two injuries during this period. On another Summers film, I had a Verey light pistol explode in my hand due to a faulty cartridge. It almost severed my thumb and broke five bones in my hand and wrist. Later, on E A Dupont’s *Cape Forlorn,* I was severely burned when a large amount of flash powder exploded spontaneously. I learned the hard way, but these unpleasant experiences made me acutely aware of the potential hazards to be encountered when using explosives and firearms.

I left BIP in 1932 and went to work at the new Ealing Studios, where I was to spend 15 happy years, particularly the eight years working with Roy Kellino after forming what was then called The Model Department, or special effects. I was encouraged by Roy to develop ideas and I designed the first hand-held fog gun, using vaporised oil. It was called a cloud machine because its main function was the production of artificial clouds for model shots. I also developed the idea of using Firefoam, and I still have the original nozzle I designed whereby snowflakes of varying sizes could be produced by simply adjusting a knurled screw. Next came the Black Burster, a pyrotechnic device with which one could produce the effect of a large explosion with a ground flash and volumes of black smoke, which looked very effective outdoors against a light sky. The explosive content in this device was half an ounce in the eight-inch diameter case, and half that in the four-inch. I think the number used to date must run into millions.

During the second half of my time at Ealing, I was mostly engaged in making and shooting miniatures for such films as *Convoy, Ships with Wings, The Bells Go Down, San Demetrio London, The Foreman Went to France* and many more. How techniques have advanced since those days. I left Ealing Studios in 1947, and I became an ACT member in the same year. Membership of the Association gave one a little prestige and I took up a three-year contract with London Films because it gave me an opportunity to work with Ned Mann, the trick expert Alexander Korda had brought over from the States to work on *The Shape of Things to Come,* and who later formed the special effects department at Worton Hall and Shepperton.

I considered it a privilege to work with Ned and I learned a lot from him, but he did have rather extravagant ideas and the large amount of money allocated by Korda was soon frittered away by overmanning and bad, bad administration. Simple trick shots became so expensive that producers avoided the department altogether, so when Ned returned to America, I

Below ‘Airship sheds in a great muddy field’ — British International Pictures’ studios in the late 1920s.

127

inherited a bankrupt department. I had no regrets when my contract expired and I hoped I'd seen Shepperton Studios for the last time. (Strangely enough, however, I was to spend some very pleasant times there later working as a freelancer).

My first film as a freelancer was *Captain Horatio Hornblower* and from then on, as the saying goes, I never looked back. In freelancing I gained a much wider experience and I saw some frightening examples of people using explosives without knowing the first thing about them - it seemed essential that some form of control be devised. When I first used high explosives in films, I was referred to by some people in the business as a dangerous man, whereas, on the contrary, high explosives, usually gelignite, was much safer to handle, because, being solid instead of in powder form, it could not be spilled and blown by the wind, and it could not be ignited by a spark. It had to be detonated. I am convinced that the use of high explosives and pre-made encased charges, such as the bursters, together with another idea of mine known as the Kicking Plate, spell safety, as well as saving production companies a vast amount of time in preparation.

Most of the films on which I worked after *Hornblower* involved the use of explosives or fires. I had a pleasant three years with Warwick Films working on *The Red Beret, High Flight, Zarak, Fire Down Below, No Time to Die* and many others. The trend was turning more and more to 'action' films and the scope for special effects widened enormously.

I was always busy and in 1962 my son John came into the business. He was keen, had good ideas and organising ability. In fact he fitted in completely. He soon became aware that an effect could be much more convincing if the artists and the crew were satisfied that there was no danger. Special effects had progressed so rapidly in a few years that for every new picture, new equipment was being designed. For example, on Sam Peckinpah's *Straw Dogs* John invented a kind of mechanical trampoline, which enabled the camera-operator to obtain a much more accurate line-up on an actor being thrown into the air by explosion or gunshot.

We also designed a much improved fire-simulating machine, which saved an enormous amount of shooting time as no preparation was necessary between takes. John also designed a special flying rig, which was used to great effect on Stanley Donen's *Little Prince.* The late Les Bowie developed a technique for matt painting, which was quicker and more accurate than previous methods. Unfortunately, Les and several other pathfinders - George Blackwell, Bill Warrington and Ted Samuels - are no longer with us, but I'm sure their contributions will be remembered for many years to come.

In the late 1960s an active Special Effects Committee within ACTT was formed and in the last five years great strides forward have been made in union-management co-operation. The formation of a joint industry committee with the Special Effects Section and the BFPTA led to the adoption of the pyrotechnic card system. Several papers are currently in preparation in an effort to make our work as safe as possible. These include codes of practice for the use of lasers, liquid petroleum gases and hazardous chemicals. The committee has also introduced a trainee system for special effects. **❜**

Above Snow effects from *Reilly 'Ace of Spies',* Thames TV's major drama production for Autumn 1983. **Below** *Moby Dick.*

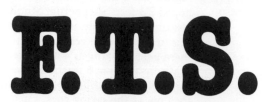
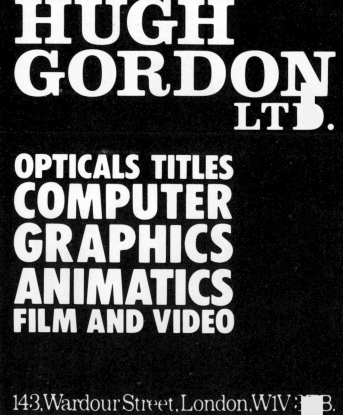

VIEW FROM THE LIGHTBOX

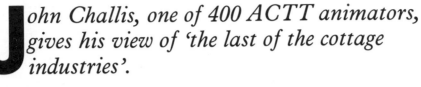

John Challis, one of 400 ACTT animators, gives his view of 'the last of the cottage industries'.

The pre-history of animation in this country goes back at least as far as the First World

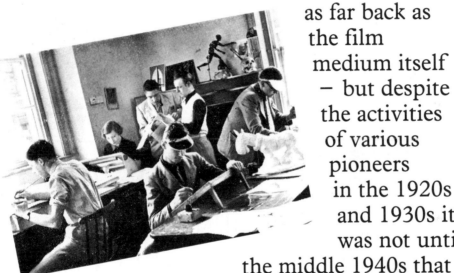

Right Animators at work in 1930.

War – almost as far back as the film medium itself – but despite the activities of various pioneers in the 1920s and 1930s it was not until the middle 1940s that anything like an animation industry emerged in response to the war-time demand for instructional and propaganda shorts. Then, as commercial television developed in the mid 1950s, the animation industry began to grow in the form in which we now recognise it, and television commercials have continued to be of fundamental importance.

Despite the occasional extra meat ration of a short, or even a feature, commercials provide most of the bread and butter for most of the animation studios, and a good deal of the particular character of the British animation scene has evolved from the interaction (and contradiction) between animation studios and advertising agencies. Animation has been described as 'the last of the cottage industries' - and students of history can find some illuminating parallels with the social and economic world of the early industrial revolution, as described by E P Thompson or Karl Marx.

Apart from one or two relatively large companies, organised more or less like factories, most of the commercial animation studios are very small - expanding or contracting according to the volume of work and often developing a speciality or house style. The majority of animation workers are freelance, doing the rounds of the studios, often working from home and having the status of sub-contractors. In these circumstances it can sometimes be hard to draw a clear distinction between employer and employee - some union members can legitimately claim to be both.

The fast turnover in jobs and people is matched by a fast turnover in styles and techniques. At its best this has fostered a variety of skills, an open-minded adaptability, an imaginative awareness of style and a readiness to experiment that are not surpassed anywhere in the world. You can get just about any kind of animation done in Britain, from the most solid traditional 1930s character animation to the most radical experiments in styles and techniques, all done to the highest professional standards. An increasing number of talented and highly qualified young workers are being attracted into the industry and standards are going up all the time.

On the other hand, this dependence on advertising also creates plenty of problems. There is a natural tendency to absorb many of the negative values of the advertising industry - becoming obsessed with 'latestness', the pursuit of the newest toys and the flashiest gimmicks at the expense of content. There is also a kind of bogus individualism that tempts us to ignore the fact that film-making is a collective activity and that gives undue prominence to the relatively few individuals at the 'creative' end of the work process, at the expense of the rest of the people doing less glamorous but equally necessary work further along the production line.

However, these are only symptoms of the fundamental problems, which can be summarised as fragmentation and lack of stability. Animators, both individually and collectively, are terribly vulnerable to the whims, fantasies, dishonesty and weak

nerves of advertisers. Even today it is still quite exceptional to find a client who really understands the medium. Fashions in advertising can change suddenly and for no particular reason - plunging us from boom into slump without warning.

Instability in the industry means insecurity for the workers in it. The animator's lifestyle could be said to be ruled by cycles - the struggle to find the next job, followed by the struggle to get it done, followed by the struggle to get well again, followed by the struggle to find the next job....and always with the not unreasonable worry that just when you're getting good at it, you find you're out of date.(Second Sod's Law - if it works it's obsolete).

Ambitious young animators, having mastered the 30-second commercial, find that they have nowhere else to go except to try to start a studio of their own in the hope of 'being able to finance their own projects from commercials', ie pull themselves up by their own bootstraps. It takes a while to realise that once on the commercial treadmill (another cycle) it's very hard to get off - since you're always running full pelt to keep up.

The best short definition of animation that I know was given a long time ago by Richard Cox who said (wagging a graphite-encrusted finger for emphasis), "The whole art of animation is to deceive the eye". Good animation is like successful conjuring - even though everyone knows logically that it's only a trick, it still seems like magic - and magic is what it's about, seducing the audience away from their familiar habits of perception, turning the world upside down and inside out and giving it a good shake. Anyone who has really mastered the art is a person deserving of the highest respect, since they should have a solid grasp of all the

resources of the medium - drawing, painting, graphics, photography, drama, poetry, music, scientific analysis and, above all, imagination and intuition.

Now, the well-tried and established techniques are being augmented and combined with the new technologies of video and computer-based image creation, extending the horizons of creative potential even further. But animation people are still frustrated by the general lack of appreciation and frequent misuse of the medium. There is a desperate need for new forms of distribution, above all, for new sources of finance. We all know that everybody loves a cartoon - the trouble is that nobody wants to pay for one. The few sponsors that do come along are usually from outside the industry and because they do not understand the medium, they have an overwhelming desire to play safe - which generally means that the magic goes straight out the window. They should be told that the one thing you can be sure of in the film industry is that playing safe is actually more of a risk than taking chances. Unfortunately, because of the timidity, blindness and greed of the majority of backers, our talents and energies continue

to be wasted on half-baked, uninspired and redundant projects. We spend too much time trying to make silk purses from sows' ears, or struggling to make dead ducks fly, or searching desperately for another small shred of meat from the dried-up carcass of the Disney system.

This may all seem very gloomy, but there are some grounds for hoping that the changes taking place in animation, and in the film industry as a whole, may be to our ultimate benefit. New technologies are offering new ways of combining images from different sources and are breaking down the habits of thought and technique that divide animation from live action, film from video, pictures from sound, and artists from technicians - as well as making everyone think harder and more adventurously about what all the others are up to. At the same time, the traditional distribution bottleneck is being challenged by an extraordinary growth in the home video market, while, though still tentative, a commendable interest is being shown by Channel 4. In this general flux, animators are beginning to overcome their isolation from other film-makers, who are in turn beginning to think of a new ways of working with animators.

Below The contemporary animator at work, as seen by John Challis.

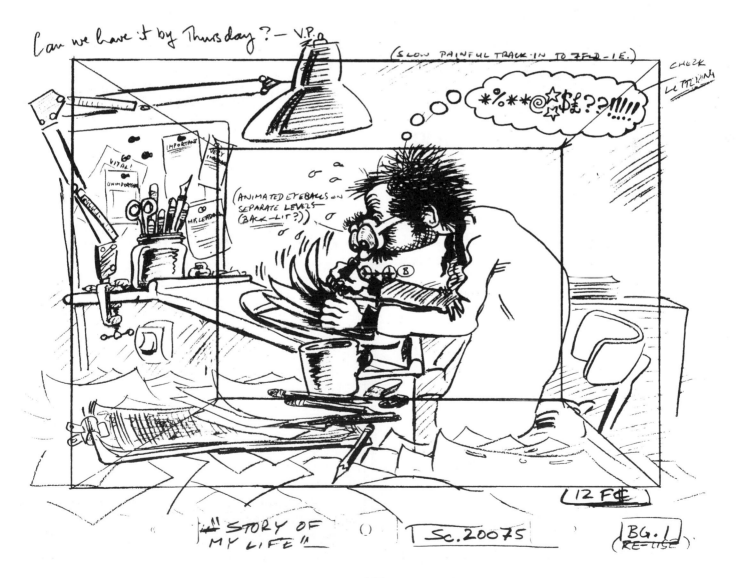

135

MODELMAKERS

J oe Telford recalls the achievements of union members in the world of the 'Wombles' and 'Paddington Bear'.

Joining in the celebrations of the union's 50th anniversary will be members whose filmic talents find their origins in the first human efforts at visual expression. I am referring, of course, to such ancient tools of the trade as the pencil, the pen and the brush, the wielders of which belong to the Animation Section and others whose talents have been extended to puppets and other inanimate objects.

Below *Alien.*

My own interest in the art spreads over many years. In fact, I well remember how, in true Tom and Jerry style, Mickey Mouse knocked Felix the Cat off the cinema screen, since it was about that time, in 1929, when I first started work as a messenger boy with a cinema publicity company. One of my tasks was to deliver four-foot-tall, cut-out figures of the famous mouse to cinemas all over London, which were then placed in the foyer when the programme included a Disney cartoon. I had to travel on public transport and was not very popular on tram, bus or train if it was getting near the rush hour.

As I continued to work in cinema poster and display studios I became aware of a mental conflict that existed among artists over tensions between their individual creativity and the need to protect their livelihood through collective trade union action. Although they joined a union they very rarely became all that active. And so it came as no surprise to me when in 1968, after I had been appointed as the organiser responsible for animation, among other things, I found that this attitude continued to prevail among animation people.

Now flat, or drawn, animation is a very labour-intensive business. But unlike live action filming, it does not require the simultaneous assembly of the unit, equipment and artistes at a given place for the production to commence. The various departments will not therefore be working together at the same time, or even in the same building. Indeed many of them may be working at home, only visiting the production office in order to collect and return their quota of work.

It will be appreciated, therefore, that it is difficult to operate an organised 'shop' within the meaning of the ACTT rule book and it will come as no surprise that this has led to problems. However, these have occurred mainly when the industry has become involved in this type of production for which it is not geared and in which managements generally have had no experience, namely animated feature films and television series.

In 1968 one such occasion arose in Soho Square, across from ACTT Head Office, when some 150 people were engaged on the production of *The Yellow Submarine*. This was set up with no pre-production meeting or consultation with head office and the whole thing appeared to be in a shambles with all manner of people, including art school students, engaged under conditions that were contrary to the union's agreements with the employer body, in this case, the British Animation Group. The anomalies included non-observance of minimum salaries, non-payment for overtime, and no holidays or holiday credits. Although attempts were made to recruit the non-members involved, it was only in the knowledge that when the production finished, most of the less skilled workers would disperse - never to be seen again unless, or until, another similar production came along.

In this particular case the union was able to redress the anomalies, but only as a result of a few hectic meetings with the American producers after they had been faced with the possibility of an incomplete film due to the threatened liquidation of the production company. A similar situation occurred during the production of *Watership Down*, even though there had been a pre-production meeting and the union had gone to considerable lengths to help the American producer to obtain work permits for some key American personnel at short notice. On this occasion one of the problems arose from the company's failure to increase salaries in line with the cost of living provisions of the agreement.

Above *Yellow Submarine.*
Below *Watership Down.*

Congratulations ACTT
50 years

VISNEWS
NEWS
PROGRAMMES
VIDEO & FILM FACILITIES

Where professionals feel at home

Above *The Wombles*. **Below**
Heads shot and edited by
EVTR for John Swinfield
Productions and Channel 4.

A further difficulty on these long-term productions arises from the fact that most animation members get their living from commercials, where their employment with a particular company can be measured in days or, occasionally, weeks. Although the prospect of many months, perhaps even a year, of regular employment on a feature may seem attractive initially, most members find the work repetitive and boring, and likely to keep them away from their commercials' connections long enough to leave them high and dry when the feature is finished. My experience tells me that the nature of the British animation industry has made those who work in it very good sprinters but not necessarily long distance runners!

In commercials, where by and large the companies are well established and the principals are also members, relationships between employees and employers are quite open and above board because any dispute could jeopardise the interests both of the advertising agencies and the clients. But the trade union organisation in the puppet and model animation side of the industry is more stable since it is normally carried out in the same manner as live-action filming, with all the unit being assembled together on the set. Perhaps one of the most well remembered puppet series was Century 21's *Thunderbirds*. While this was filmed as ordinary live action, rather than stop frame animation, nevertheless the Animation Section of ACTT was represented by the puppeteers who manipulated the puppets from a gantry above the miniature sets. Incidentally, I believe this production

stimulated the development of lip-synching techniques for the puppets' dialogue.

Since those days there have been numerous other series and individual programmes produced mostly for children's TV. It was about ten years ago when *The Wombles* made their first appearance, subsequently to be followed by *Paddington Bear.* This series has the interesting feature of a three-dimensional main character supported by single-plane secondary characters cut from cardboard and designed for limited movement. A further aspect of such series is the spin-off on merchandising that occurs. No doubt it could be argued that this enables such series to continue successfully.

The term 'model' as opposed to puppet can cover any inanimate object which, through the use of stop-motion photography, can be made to appear to move. It has been used on cut-out shapes of every kind of material and was widely used in the early days of television advertising with all manner of products, including cigarettes, confectionery and razor blades. Today, the repertoire has been extended and indeed the technique is used so subtly that it may be hardly noticed!

Most of the present grades in the Animation Section were included in the first Shorts and Documentaries Agreement between the union and the Association of Specialised Film Producers in 1942, when the shorts industry had already established a reputation for the high quality of its productions for the Ministry of Information during the Second World War. This standard has continued in industrial short films, with special contributions from diagram and lettering artists, and the experience of all grades in cinema advertising contributed to the success of commercial TV when it was launched in the 1950s.

The formal relationship between the union and the employers through working agreements has eradicated the mental conflict for individuals that I have referred to, and recent Annual Conference agendas confirm that the Animation Section now fully participates in the affairs of the union.

So, in celebrating this fiftieth anniversary, ACTT can feel proud of the contribution made by its Animation members to British film-making, with such productions as *Animal Farm, The Little Island* and *A Christmas Carol.*

In joining in these celebrations, Animation Section members, I am sure, appreciate the fact that for more than 30 of these 50 years they have worked under agreements that include index-linked pay scales - no mean achievement for a comparatively small union during a period dominated by wage restraint and (official or unofficial) pay policies.

DO YOU NЕED
TO KNOW EVERYTHING
IN TELEVISION?

THEN SUBSCRIBE TO TELEVISION WEEKLY
and get the headlines every week

ED TECH

*E*ducational technology brought a new
dimension to learning and a new branch to
the union. Bob Hamilton reports.

The creation of, as they were then called,
Education Television Units in the mid-1960s, led ACTT's General
Council to form an ETV
Sub-Committee in June
1967 with representatives
from the three branches.
Parallel to this, the
Television Branch also
formed a sub-committee,
mainly as a result
of existing members
moving into ETV and
requesting continuity of their ACTT

Right Mobile TV unit.
Below A stage in the fight
against the closure of GTVS.

membership. In January 1968, the union
for the first time appointed
an organiser with specific
responsibility for this
new field, and following
this it was agreed
to amalgamate the
two committees and to
create an ETV Section
that was directly
under the control
of General Council
and independent of the branches.
A widespread recruitment campaign

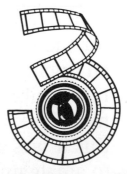

followed and membership of the Section reached three figures within weeks. This, in turn, led to the creation of ETV shops at the Centre for Educational Television Overseas, at Leeds University and at Coventry Corporation. Other shops followed as the membership increased, with representatives from the shops serving on the ETV Committee. The honour of being the first shop went to CETO in St John's Wood, with the redoubtable Lyn Robinson as shop steward. Lyn was also to be the first chairperson of the committee and its early successes were due, in no small measure, to her experience and enthusiasm, with representatives from the three branches also providing solid ACTT background to the recently recruited stewards and organiser. In May 1969, it was agreed that the term ETV had outlived its usefulness and the Section became the Educational Technology Section.

It must be said that ACTT's interest in the new field was not universally welcomed, with the traditional educational unions not taking kindly to our intervention in an area they regarded as purely an extension of existing educational techniques. To be fair, these unions have no inconsiderable record of organisation in a notoriously difficult field. The first years of the new organisation were therefore characterised by a series of inter-union problems, meetings at the TUC and recognition demands being resisted by the already recognised unions, the latter being a situation that persists to the present day.

Despite the opposition, members continued to be recruited and shops established as the area expanded - remember these were the days of the Harold Wilson technological revolution, and while recognition was difficult to achieve, ACTT shops evolved local negotiating procedures and often found ingenious ways round the lack of national recognition. A most useful and mutually beneficial relationship was established in 1970 with the National Educational Closed Circuit Television Association (NECCTA). Joint ventures included a number of publications, perhaps the most notable being *Staffing and Training in Educational Closed Circuit Television,* which was to remain for some years as the standard work in this field. As the membership gained experience of trade unionism in general, and ACTT in particular, the role of the representatives from the branches became less and less significant and indeed from 1971 the Section members were by and large left to handle their own affairs.

The union's Rules Revision Conference of 1974 created a new fourth branch, the Educational Technology Branch, which held its inaugural meeting on 6 July 1974. It is always dangerous to give a list of prominent members; nevertheless, mention must be made of the three original chairpersons of the Section - Lyn Robinson, Stan Walker and Brenda Morrison.

Right Brighton Polytechnic Media Production Services on location at a primary school.

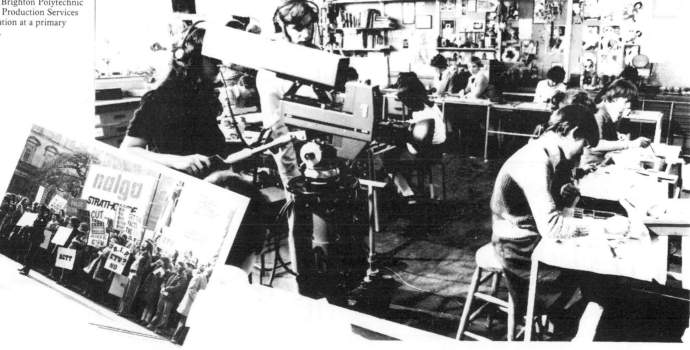

BBH Broadcast Hire

We believe we have become the largest "dry-hire" Outside Broadcast facilities company in the U.K. with the addition to our existing fleet of our latest "flag-ship"; a 3-camera van with mobile VTR and on-board 12.5kVA fully sound-proofed generator. With our well-known existing facilities of a one-camera with VTR van, a two-camera with VTR van, a Volvo Estate and Ford Cortina for our "E.N.G. EQUIPMENT"; we now offer for hire a comprehensive range of E.N.G. and E.F.P. facilities complemented by a new Service Van for carrying camera cables, technical equipment etc.

A brief description follows of the technical facilities provided by the 3-camera unit:-

3-Camera OB Unit

The vehicle is based on a Mercedes 608D chassis, is **Fully Air-conditioned** and has a **Roof Mounted Camera Platform** with **Tripod Mounts** and **Safety Guard Rail**. It incorporates it's own **Onboard Fully Sound-Proofed 12.5kVA Generator** permitting complete freedom to shoot wherever you choose with a simple lighting system.

Cameras

The **Three Hitachi SK91** camera channels with the latest **Triax Control Units** allow each camera a working range of **Up to 4000ft from the unit**. Normally fitted with the Fujinon 14 x 9 lens, there is now the added facility of a 30 x 11 lens complete with **Five Shot Box, Servo Focus** and **Servo Zoom**.

Vision

Full Broadcast Specifications: 1" C Format **VTR**, 8-Channel Cox **Vision Mixer, Dual SPG, Off-Air Monitoring** and **Test Signals**.

Audio

The audio side is based on the **Audix MXT 1000 Ten-Channel Sound Desk** and **Ferrograph Logic Recorder** with **Full Monitoring, Patching** and **Talkback Facilities.**

With it's **Link 1098 Caption Scanner** and **Barco Off-Air Receiver** (using the **Clark Hydraulic Mast**) the vehicle is a very comprehensively fitted-out OB Van.

We are located at Newbury in Berkshire; a 24-hour answering service is provided.
"BBH Broadcast Hire" is a totally owned division of Personnel & Electronics Limited with its head office at Hayes in Middlesex, near to London Airport.

Please contact us either on **Newbury (0635) 45124** or **Hayes 01-573 8333** for further information or if you prefer to telex, our number is **934271**

PERSONNEL & ELECTRONICS LTD.

Triumph House   1096 Uxbridge Road
Hayes   Middlesex   UB4 8QH   England   U.K.

Telephone: 01-573 8333   Telex: 934271

LOCAL AIR

obin Blake, ACTT shop steward at London's Capital Radio, traces the ten-year-old chequered story of independent local radio, 'whose pot of gold has been found to be less than half full'.

The 50th anniversary of ACTT happens to fall on another notable birthday – October 1983 marks ten years from Capital Radio's first broadcast to London. London is the only region to be allotted two independent local radio stations – LBC handles a news and information franchise, while Capital occupies the more lucrative music and entertainments slot. Both stations ultimately founded ACTT shops, but Capital's was in many ways unusual. Its foundation constituted something of a case history in modern trade unionism.

The Capital ACTT shop was the creation of a few far-thinking early members, and of National Organiser, Bob Hamilton, who put in hundreds of hours between them in setting it up. The shop didn't take root without a struggle. It was evident quite early to most staff that some form of union would be needed. But

148

management, if not actually hostile, was inexperienced in industrial relations and found it hard to swallow the practical suggestions (let alone demands) of representatives of the members. But suggestions and demands there had to be, since, although ACTT had been recognised as a negotiating body, no agreed minimum terms and conditions existed as the station went on air. These were hammered out during a hard year's negotiating, and later formed the basis for many subsequent agreements inside ILR.

The open-shop principle - insisted on by the early members - was also unpopular with the company. Originally, no doubt, recognition had been intended to embrace technical grades only. But the shop was determined to recruit in all departments and at all grades, a policy which alone is responsible for the size and influence of the Capital shop today. This stands at almost 70 members. Management could offer no convincing counter argument to the open shop, while the officers were able

to demonstrate clear advantages in the establishment of published grades across the board, minimum rates and conditions, a clear disputes procedure and representation of members' interests by shop officers who cared enough to get results.

From its earliest days, the Capital shop was also concerned for the wider issues of

broadcasting. ILR was a brand-new industry. Operational principles were theoretically enshrined in the Broadcasting Act and the IBA rules, but were as yet untested in practice. A clear understanding by union members of their responsibilities to the public was required - a responsibility to establish good custom and practice that would marry public service with the working interests of the staff. In fact, the fist major dispute hinged on a public issue.

The company had acquired an American machine (the Shaefer) that would enable unmanned broadcasting. It was proposed that this should be introduced overnight, with taped programmes replacing live presentation. ACTT had never organised Capital's presenters, and the company was not proposing to abolish the technicians' night shift. But the shop took the view that this was a breach of the station's franchise (which had promised 24-hour, live broadcasting) and refused to co-operate, blacking the automatic equipment). For weeks, Capital was off the air between midnight and 6am. In the end management relented. The Shaefer machine was consigned to gathering dust

in a corner of the MCR, and live broadcasting round the clock was resumed.

It was a point worth establishing because ILR had come in on a wave of enthusiasm for the ideals of the common touch and audience involvement. Early ILR franchise applications vied with each other to have more community-based ideas, feedback, access, and public service. Often, these ideas may have been cynically motivated, but their power to

convince the IBA and (at first) the public was undoubted. However it proved to be a policy that was hard to translate into programming. In particular, the 'community radio' idea, as exemplified at Cardiff and elsewhere, has been very much more problematic than originally projected. The problem is, perhaps, in the legislation. This requires ILR stations to be wholly self-financing which in practice has meant through advertising revenue. However, commercial, conventional ILR stations have found that a community radio stance is not likely to lead to mass audiences, and that their love affair with the advertising fraternity has consequently cooled down.

At Cardiff, a community trust occupies seats on the board, with community broadcasting an integral part of the station's franchise. Cardiff in its early results, illustrated the difficulty. In three years it accumulated a loss of £223,000. A way of harmonising professional, community and commercial considerations is needed if ILR is to succeed in these areas. Significant

numbers of other ILR stations - community or otherwise - have had trouble attracting sufficient revenue. In addition the gap between rich and poor stations has grown wider. This makes attempts to reach national agreements all the more difficult.

But while the poor companies get poorer, the richer companies are not unruffled by the cold wind of recession. The true effect is unfortunately being felt

(or heard) in programming. Programme controllers have gambled that more conservative programming will boost advertisers' confidence without losing the audience. I would argue that audiences will be lost through this policy.

ILR was launched on an adventurous ticket - a promise of exciting radio that could tap new audiences. A backtracking on that promise must alienate audiences, or at least inhibit audience growth - low revenue being the inevitable consequence. ILR was originally intended to claim a five to eight per cent share of national advertising revenue. But the total share has now stuck short of three per cent. The pot of gold at the end of the ILR rainbow has been found to be less than half full.

But this pessimism must not obscure the real achievements of ILR. Stolid though much of it is, it has nevertheless carried forward the revolution started by the illegal offshore pirates if only haltingly. It has added a new local dimension to public broadcasting, and has provided many imaginative and useful services. Some of its innovations have been durable enough to be copied in other media. In the field of industrial relations, ILR has seen one of the most potentially far reaching developments of recent years.

As a result of much hard work by ACTT National Organiser Noel Harris, and his opposite members in the NUJ and the ABS, the negotiating Alliance of Commercial Radio Unions was formed in 1982. The Alliance's first objective - to present a united front in negotiations with the employers, was achieved in the first few months. A single national agreement for all clerical, technical, production and journalistic staff is the next aim. After that - who knows? The Alliance may well develop as the seed of that single broadcasting/entertainments union that so many people see as the only hope for an effective trade union presence in those areas.

I hope that all ACTT shops in commercial radio will help to build on this achievement. I hope they will press forward on all fronts indicated in this sketch; that they will work to make their product more responsible and more exciting; that they will forge and protect links with other groups of workers in their own and in similar industries; and, above all, I hope they will keep before them the importance of uniting around grassroots issues. A shop is surely founded on the good casework of its officers, and this work must be supported by the united membership of shops. The shop at Capital would not exist in its present form and its present strength if this had not been realised by the early pioneers - people like Charles Kennedy, Mike Sykes and Brenda Marshall. I believe that in the 50th anniversary year of ACTT the union owes them a great deal.

YORKSHIRE TELEVISION

The Television Centre, Leeds LS3 1JS

BOTANIST ON THE BRIDGE

Alan Sapper is ACTT's General Secretary and much else besides. Sue Hayes discovered what makes him tick.

Alan Sapper's mum would be proud of him, for her advice was to get a secure, professional job with prospects. At 17, he did just what she said and joined the civil service.

As a civil servant, he took a part-time external degree in botany and the 'much more difficult' Kew Gardens Certificate. He worked at Kew as a taxonomic botanist. Later, he decided to apply for the job as the Assistant to the General Secretary of ACTT, George Elvin.

However, if ACTT hadn't given him the job, today he may well have been the leader of the Guild of Insurance Officers. For, on the same day as he faced the interview panel of among others, Alf Cooper, Charlie Wheeler, Frank Fuller, Ralph Bond, Sid Cole, Ken Gordon, Monica Toye and Max Anderson, he also had an interview as London Secretary to the Insurance Officers' Guild.

Above Half a century of General Secretaryship between them — George Elvin and Alan Sapper at the 1983 ACTT Annual Conference. **Right** Alan Sapper receives the Bell of Congress from Alan Fisher after completing his presidency of the TUC, September 1982.

A house in Soho Square

The union has had three homes - 30 Piccadilly Mansions (behind the old Bovril sign that used to dominate the Circus), 145 Wardour Street and 2 Soho Square. (There was also an interregnum when the union functioned from George Elvin's parents' home at Stanmore as the bombs were falling around London).

It was in 1947, after the end of the Second World War, that the union acquired the freehold of Number 2 for a song - £18,000. For another song it could have bought the building right through to Dean Street. But the members, erring on the side of prudence, decided against such a rash purchase, which would have solved a lot of subsequent problems as the union grew.

Soho Square was laid out in 1681 and Number 2 is one of the few houses remaining that is identifiable from the original design. It was on this square that the ill-fated Duke of Monmouth had his palace (on the south side, where the hospital now stands). His followers cried, "Sohoe", as they went to death and defeat on the field of Sedgemoor in 1685.

Over the last 300 years the square has had associations as diverse as the film industry itself. Disreputable aristocracy repaired to 'The White House' at Number 20 (then the most ornate brothel in town), while on the opposite corner, Sir Joseph Banks, President of the Royal Society, turned his house at Number 30 (now part of the 20th Century Fox Building) into 'a sort of academy of science - a rallying point for men of science and genius of all countries'. Number 2 had its own distinguished period nearly 200 years ago as the London embassy of the Venice City State. Presumably, the ambassador held court in Alan Sapper's pine-pannelled room, where nearly four decades of F & GP Committee meetings have now been held. After the Venetian ambassador there were less salubrious residents - it is said that Number 2 was on the direct route of one of London's principal rat runs. Like the early British film-makers, the rats were going west.

Today, any ACTT member who sits on the grass of the square to eat his or her sandwiches, may do so with a proprietorial air not shared by your common-or-garden visitor to Soho. The freeholder of Number 2 owns one thirty-second part of the square itself.

Peter Avis

Left ACTT staff allow themselves a few moments' distraction so that Wolf Suschitzky can capture them on film. (From left to right and top to bottom) Doreen Burt, Jane Creaney, Sarah Courtney, Jacki McCarten, Glen O'Connor, Amanda Denning, Alan Sapper, John Lloyd, Pat Nicholas, Sandra Horne, Maureen Whyte, Jackie Sinclair, Ken Roberts, Norman Sutcliffe, Lorna Nicholas, George Maniatakis, Bobbie Osterley, Joyce Bradshaw, Peter Avis, Marina Hale, Jenny Eager, Anne McLoughlin, Yvonne Hill, Pauline Wiles, Deborah Snell, Phyllis Grant, Lynda Loakes, Jo Fontana, Geoff Conway, Andy Egan, Roy Lockett.

Unavoidably absent from the photocall in May 1983 were: Rebecca Annadale, Carol Aviet, Anita Flynn, Bob Hamilton, Noel Harris, Brenda Juggins, Janice Kyprou, Anne McFarlane, Jacqui Mulder, Jack O'Connor, Nick Salmon, Brian Shemmings, Alec Telford, Les Wiles.

He was in fact, offered both posts. But, says Sapper, 'The decision on which job to accept was an easy one'. His real answer, to that standard interviewer's question, 'Why do you want this job?', although not necessarily the one he gave at the time, was that he had a secret ambition to write and make films. Just then, his spare time was taken up by writing and directing for the 88 Film Group. The group made medical training films on such subjects as childbirth and mental health as well as featurettes, 'which were bloody awful' and policiées,

which were 'good fun'. He also wrote TV scripts, articles, short stories and plays. One of his plays, *The Return*, was performed by the Hovel Theatre Group, a theatre for actors.

To a certain extent, Alan Sapper regarded the job as Assistant to the General Secretary as a fulfilment of his desire to serve the Labour movement. For then, like now, he believed that 'film and television are extremely important to democratic expression'. In 1958 he started working for ACTT where he quickly gained a reputation for saying what he thought. 'I got up the noses of people then.' Even now, he likes people who say what they think, he can't cope with whingers who moan on not saying what they really mean. But saying what one thinks is often a sign of someone who is angry or dissatisfied. Alan would say that it was because he was a rebel and always had been since he was a young boy. Maybe this is due to his family background.

He grew up as the youngest of three boys. His mother, Kate Williams, was a suffragette who had gone to prison for her beliefs. She had grown up in the West End of London. 'Indeed, she knew about the Soho area very well. She used to tell us stories about the Crosse & Blackwell factory just around the corner from Soho Square and also about the soap factory in

Hanway Place.' Apparently, the fumes were so bad, they used to make people ill. 'So even before I worked for ACTT I knew this area. Today, I'm overlooking a square that was in my dreams.' By trade, his mother was a seamstress and 'in her trade, women were only allowed to do button-hole seams, never pressing and cutting....'. She was forced to take in piece-work when his father, a book-keeper, was out of work due to ill health. 'It was then that I first became aware, or began to realise that there was something wrong, or there was a different structure to be achieved.'

He has two brothers, Peter who is an accountant and Laurie who retired as General Secretary of the Association of University Teachers in April 1983. Laurie is his eldest brother, and the one he is closest to. 'He was my surrogate father, when I was growing up.' At 14 Laurie ran away to join the International Brigade, but was returned home by two policemen. His influence and views appear to have sown the first seeds of Alan Sapper's discontent with the status quo. Even today he will proudly tell you endless stories about Laurie and his achievements. In all he thinks he's a 'fantastic bloke'.

On leaving school Alan Sapper joined the civil service, where he became active in the Institution of Professional Civil Servants. He was first elected as section secretary and then took staff association leave to become a full-time branch secretary. However, his promotion within the civil service was blocked because of his union activities and it was then that he decided to leave.

As a taxonomic botanist he is an Associate Licentiate of the Linnean Society. The General Secretary of ACTT has a particular interest in *Epilobium Angustifolium* - the fireweed that is spread across the Canadian forest - which he first

encountered as a boy in the London Blitz. 'Fireweed grows very well on burned down buildings', he says. In the botanical world, Alan Sapper's modest claim to fame is in having introduced *Tolpis Barbata*, a member of the daisy family he spotted in Yugoslavia, to the Royal Botanical Gardens. He gathered some seeds 30 years ago, and now the ochre and mauve flower is a permanent resident in the herbaceous border at Kew. You can find it in the official list with the note, 'Introduced by Sap'. Even today his fascination with botany continues. His garden has been given over to nature - he does little tending, preferring to see what will eventually happen. He is married to a doctor and they have two children, both students. He likes to keep his home-life private and for relaxation his hobby, apart from the plants, is music, classical and jazz. He recently lost his categorisation as a judo brown belt. 'My aim is still to get a First Dan before I am too old', he says. (He is a vigorous 52-year-old in 1983). But the truth is that he doesn't have too much

Above Soho Square in about 1700. ACTT's future home is bottom right.

usually gets into his office at about nine, 'unless there is an early morning meeting'. From then on, he scan-reads five or six newspapers, does his mail, organises his diary with Lorna Nicholas, his secretary, reads the latest statistics and then begins the long round of meetings with individuals and committees. 'Do you know, I've seen representatives from every country in the world in my office?' His committee work is ferocious. He is a member of at least 25 . He also tries to make time for anyone who wants to talk to him. 'I try to have an open-door policy, but it is not often possible.' Very little throws Alan Sapper, but when he does get angry, his anger is directed at those who think he is the ultimate power over communications in the UK. 'What they don't realise is how little power I have. My members have all the power.'

Alan Sapper has made his mark on the film and broadcasting industry in many ways. He is a founder member of the Confederation of Entertainment Unions, which gave rise to the Federation of Film Unions. He has been a member of the

Below From *Un Cartoon de Alan Parker*. © Alan Parker Film Company, Pinewood Studios.

time these days for throwing the odd opponent around the gym - hence his recent slip down the judo ladder. But, he does exercise for 20 minutes every day. 'They are a mixture of strengthening, relaxing and stretching exercises from the Health Education Council and Judo, as well as one exercise from the *Jane? Fonda Body Work-Out Book.*'

He became ACTT's General Secretary in 1969, and enjoys the phenomenal amount of work the job requires. He

You see Mr Marshall Here we do things a little differently to your Mr Sapper....

'Shoot the Moon' '81

Cinematograph Films Council since the early 1970s and he is a director of the Children's Film Foundation (being particularly proud of a three-year campaign he led to prevent its closure). Other industry jobs include being a governor of the British Film Institute and a governor of the National Film and Television School. And, beyond these shores, there is his presidency of FISTAV, the International Federation of Audio-Visual Workers Unions.

Something of a stormy petrel in British politics, he has views on such matters as disarmament and the Common Market that are well-known or, some would say, notorious. 'I am a passionate peacemonger and a passionate anti-Marketeer', he says. Indeed, he is a founder member of the Campaign for Nuclear Disarmament and a founder member and Chairman of Trade Unions Against the Common Market. While he gives his own flavour to political pronouncements, he is pleased to be able to say that the views he expresses on the main issues are in line with the conference policies of his own union and of the Trades Union Congress.

First elected a member of the TUC General Council in 1969, he became its Chairman for 1982-83. It was a job he

obviously enjoyed.

Alan Sapper admits that he is always being asked what he will do next. Will he, for example, go into parliamentary politics? He is a life-long member of the Labour Party, not necessarily because he agrees with all it has done in office, but 'because it is the party of the masses'. However, he doesn't think his career is likely to take a Westminster direction. He would only consider accepting a cabinet post in a Labour government as Minister for Communications.

For the present, looking beyond ACTT's 50th anniversary, he looks forward to being involved in some more solid achievements on behalf of his union and its members. He wants to see one amalgamated media union, a cross-industry pension scheme, residual payments for all members, a much stronger FISTAV with a full-time research staff and ACT Films becoming a fully established multi-media production company. And he adds, 'We must pay a much higher regard to the quality of life of people working in our industry - particularly we have to deal with the problems of stress and alcoholism'.

ACTT's General Secretary has a full agenda for the future.

Everyone shows old films from Hollywood. We finance new British ones as well.

Don't get us wrong about American movies, there's no way we'd be without them.

But at Channel 4, we believe in the British film industry too.

We've already commissioned twenty new British feature films, and there are plenty more to come.

Michael Apted, Ian McKewan, Sarah Miles, David Puttnam, Jack Rosenthal and Janet Suzman are just a few of the people making movies with us.

We commission our television programmes too, giving valuable work to the British independent sector, and getting terrific quality in return.

The same kind of quality that's earned our films impressive reviews on the big screen.

Who knows, we could be the first television company to win an Oscar.

CHANNEL FOUR TELEVISION.

TOMORROW TODAY

And so the challenges of the 1980s and beyond. Roy Lockett finds the prospect exciting, and calls for 'a new model to meet new social and democratic priorities'.

Above Roy Lockett (centre) on a visit with Labour MPs to Shepperton film studios, 1982.

Founded relatively late in an erratic industry dominated for much of its history by American investment and marketing power, ACTT has evolved into a curiously hybrid union. Hated and loved, periodically a cockpit of ferocious industrial, cultural and political conflict, it has been in the ring for 50 years in which time its opponents – and sometimes its supporters – have slugged away at it unmercifully.

It has never been low profile. First, because it couldn't be – the work of its members pierces every sector of British society – and second, because it didn't want to be. Industrially, politically and culturally, the union has always adopted clear and often controversial postures.

And around those policies a fringe of myth has flourished, giving an often welcome aura of mysterious power.

Fifty years is a long time in a young industry - from the ecstatic and profitable crowds pouring out of first screenings of the new talkies to an age of footprints, acorn surveys and Japanese VCRs. The history of the union is a number of histories. A history of the labour movement, a cultural history, a political and economic history and a technical history. Elsewhere in the book these themes - bumping and scraping together - are explored in more detail. They are of major importance and transfixing interest. There is, however, another history that is richer and more specific than these - a psychological and sociological history. Thousands and thousands of activists arguing, working and stretching themselves in the search for an organisation, activities and policies, that would meet their needs and sometimes their dreams.

The richness of this history - the thousands of individual trajectories from which men and women have entered and shaped and reshaped the union - is one we ignore at our peril. There is an assiduously fostered view that unions, their officials and members are grey, homogenous and disciplined groups dully treading a common and unremarkable path. It is a vulgar and anti-humanist caricature. In a democratic structure - and whatever its enemies have ever said of ACTT they cannot say it is not that - the fertilising and explosive interaction of personality, background, occupation and personal beliefs has been the core of energy from which the union and all its works have been generated. Our history is a dialogue between individuals and ideas. Those swirling convection currents are still in motion.

From the early women stewards who predated the energising force of a resurgent feminism - running their shops like huge extended families - to the ferocious advocates of the revolutionary cause of 1930's documentarianism, to the tough cookies who built a rock-like union in the newest industry of ITV in the mid-1950s, to the stature of George Elvin casting his giant shadow across 40 years of an industry's history - all of these have moulded the growth of the union. Each with different patterns of social and political commitment, different priorities and fears - able to work together in a union with the imagination and confidence to place power where it belongs - at the bottom.

It is in that diversity and the collectivist structure in which it operates, that the liberating effect of trade unionism is located. A school of the hardest knocks where the support of others is hard earned and hard argued.

Where the confidence of your peers grows upon the rock of ability, relevance and utility. A life in which unanimity is extraordinary and debate the precondition for action. The living expression of democracy.

But democracy does not spring up naturally like the daffodils in spring. Nor does power - the power of thousands and thousands acting together. In a world of massive commercial and political power blocs, of unemployment, fear, exploitation and, often, a paralysing apathy - the union was created in the Britain of the 1930s. Only the mad or the self-interested can see no parallels with the Britain of the 1980s. From a fragmented, crazily overworked industry, dominated commercially and culturally by America, a small group of men and women with their only resource imagination and the historical lessons of a 100-year-old labour movement, bricked together the foundations of their own organisation. A set of policies was defined early and largely achieved with resolution and panache by the end of the Second World War.

Early strategies

Early strategies were clear. The need for a powerful industrial base of organisation with the attendant merits of basic working-class 'nous'. Film processing became a clear priority. By the end of the 1930s, this element in the strategy had been achieved. Next, the equally difficult task of organising film production workers - from clapper loader to director. Hard, very hard. Brilliant manoeuvering and a sure foot in the corridors of power by Elvin and the astonishing Anthony Asquith, first union President of patrician family and in the 1930s ranked with Hitchcock as one of the industry's twin directorial hopes, then ensured that at the outbreak of war, the government did not quietly close down the film industry and lock the door behind them. Somehow they achieved government agreement that ACTT membership was essential for recognition as a film technician by the armed services. Membership leapt. After that nothing could stop it.

With Quota - defended in an earlier ACTT campaign - protecting British film production in cinemas and in 1948 the young Harold Wilson's enthusiastic creation of the National Film Finance Corporation and the invention of the Eady Levy, the only remaining object of that early strategy was a National Film School. Through the Lloyd Committee, on which Elvin was a driving force, the National Film School surged into existence. Often caught in a flux of argument about elitism, under the astute political control of Colin Young, it has fed its distinctive and employment generating alumni into film and television.

Throughout this period the union grappled with the shrinking indigenous base of British feature production. Since its bold inception in the late 1940s, the NFFC has dwindled into insignificance as a source of finance for British features. While the lusty infants of television film production, commercials and sponsored filming developed a degree of autonomy rooted in regulated public broadcasting, advertising, marketing and education, features have largely remained a service industry for the American majors. Occasionally, brave attempts have been made to challenge this dependency. Michael Balcon at Woodfall films with *Saturday Night and Sunday Morning, This Sporting Life* and other ground-breaking movies, the golden age of

Right Albert Finney in *Saturday Night and Sunday Morning.*

the Ealing comedies, even Bryan Forbes' brief rule at Elstree with a programme of British films - all of these leaked into insignificance in the infinite absorbency of the Americans' domination of the world market in making and screening movies.

Survival or extinction

Two major union attempts were made in the 1950s and the 1970s to dynamite the

log-jam of American domination. The first was argued in *Survival or Extinction,* a bold plan to create a third publicly-owned cinema circuit linked to a studio base. The aim was a genuinely British sector with enough clout to compete with Rank and ABC (now EMI) in the marketplace. The initiative raised interest and enthusiasm but Macmillan's government remained unmoved. The second frontal assault on the industry's multinational power blocs was *Nationalising the Film Industry,* a detailed research report that argued unequivocally for public ownership of the entire industry - production, distribution and exhibition - under democratic control. The furore which this revolutionary demand caused resounded through the union evoking passionate support and ferocious opposition. At the end of the day, the Labour government remained unmoved.

There is a three-fold argument against total dependence on America. The first is cultural. Britain's directors, writers and film-makers are working to the remit of Americans who make films for the world market. They rarely embody or examine the preoccupations, history and richness of British society. Ours is not a national cimema. The second critique of the dependence on America rests on profits. While the UK benefits from the studio and facilities hire and employment incomes generated by American dollars, their huge earnings - *Alien, Superman, Star Wars* - enrich the American economy, not the British. Most significantly, they impart a deep, almost hysterical instability to movie output and therefore to the employment of British actors, crafts persons, technicians and industry resources. It is a cycle of boom and slump; feast and famine.

methods for reporting TV news pictures to our homes in such a short space of time; he will look further. He is masterminding a marriage for his brainchild. Not peculiarly enough with its old broadcast television counterpart, but with film.

Electronic Field Production amounts to a small reliable television camera and recorder on location; in film terms an Arriflex and Nagra. But it carries around with it a laboratory, and it is this, its supreme advantage for news gathering, which is its Achilles heel for features. Its automated functions continually deal in averages and compromises to the exclusion of anything special. It provides a limited set of options rather than a means of pure expression; it needs ingenuity to extend its qualities for the feature.

Panavision is the latest to lend a hand, offering its standard range of lenses and filters to improve the image of video circuitry.

Bright young film-makers are testing the new technology in a series of experiments designed to enhance the video image and take advantage of it. They call for changes which everyone must respond to.

Video, currently practised by the 'video boutiques', needs more 'string and sealing wax' about it, as with film; someone to scratch a bit of glass for the technology to work on to produce flare.

The fashion should be for the product, not just the tools, thereby creating a uniqueness and developing styles of programme making. We can look to manufacturers for continued electronic advancement which will offer more and more possibilities to movie makers. It doesn't mean we must join a rat race of micro circuitry which limits our efforts by its very intrusion.

All this places stresses on the movie making industry generally. Suddenly no-one can find staff. What price a video tape editor? Or an engineer?

Cable is coming, of course, and satellite too. No one may have satisfactorily resolved the economics of these developments, but video is immensely fashionable and there are very few fashionable investment opportunities. It will not be passed by. And how will facilities companies, which will grow to become the largest producers of programming in a diverse marketplace, adapt to the call for more programmes to be shown to fewer people and therefore be made for less money. It doesn't mean they will not prosper. Lots of businesses run very well by the efficient production of high volume, low-cost products. But will this industry carry on the traditions of the film industry to nurture new approaches and make better and better movies; will it make a *Chariots of Fire*?

The technology is certainly capable of doing so, given expert and caring application, for with people and video it is possible to do more than with people and celluloid. We shall need 'bespoke tailoring' rather more than fitting together a selection of arms, zips and pocket flaps. It is a great opportunity. But only with the help of those pillars of the industry which have been pushed around during the change, because the union and its membership are best placed to nurture the potential of this bright, clever, teenager.

Melvyn Kirner

Below Marlon Brando (centre) and Susannah York (right) in *Superman* - do such American megafilms contribute to the cycle of boom and slump, feast and famine?

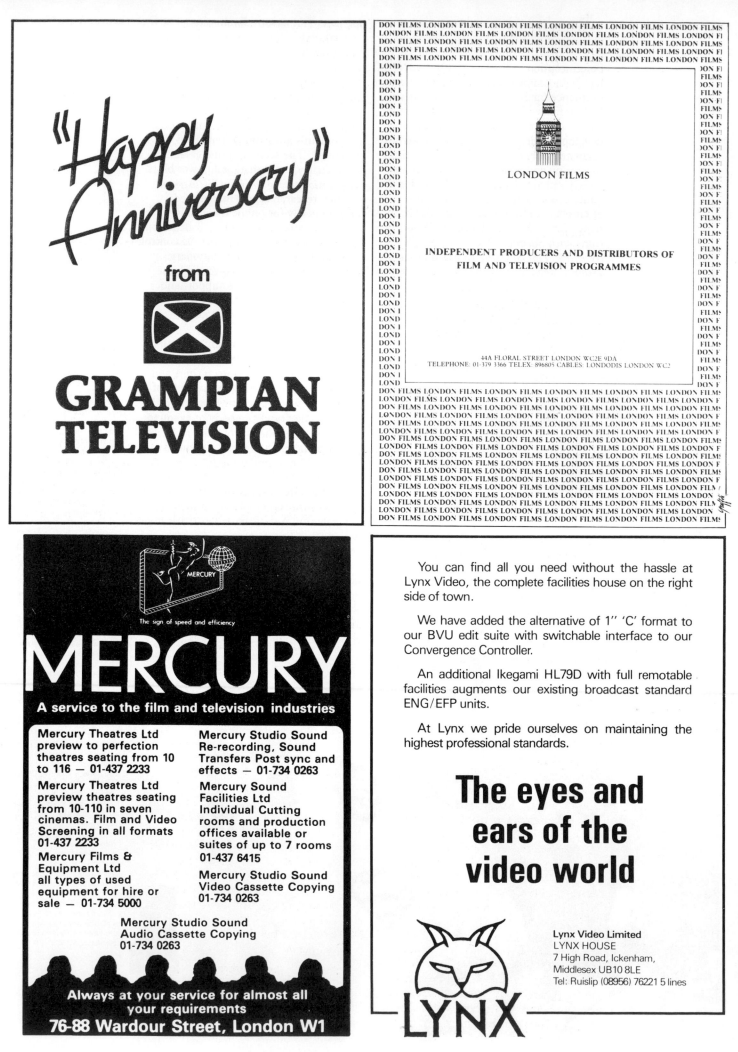
162

Boom and slump

In the long boom of the 1960s - largely due to American investment - the production of features doubled, reaching an extraordinary peak in 1968. American cash flooded in. British films were big business in the world's box offices. Somehow randy *Tom Jones* caught the flavour of the swinging 60s. But the boom collapsed. In a few months, the Vietnam war and a slump on Wall Street saw crashing levels of British production. We ended the 1960s with the same number of features we'd made at the start of the decade. The problem was that in response to the boom, ACTT's film membership had doubled. Double the members, half the work. The result was massive unemployment. Shatteringly, this coincided with economic turmoil in ITV where the new Yorkshire franchise loaded huge additional costs onto ITV without increasing advertising revenue and a sharp drop in commercials output rooted in the ban on cigarette advertising. For two or three years the industry was on its knees. Risking oversimplification, that pattern of boom and slump continued into the 1980s. From mid 1982, the level of feature production rose strongly. In early 1983, the short-term position looked excellent. But it is always the short-term.

Here it is crucial to enter two caveats. First, the British industry - and our union in particular - welcomes American investment. It provides employment and income. It provides technical and creative challenges that have been central to stimulating the astonishing expertise which the UK has developed from the script conference, through casting and art department, to sound, production and camera on the floor - not forgetting our magnificent SFX specialists - to editing, dubbing and film processing. We would be a technically impoverished industry had US investment not periodically flooded our industry.

A cultural pivot

The *But* swings on a cultural pivot. With nothing approaching the resources and regulatory structure of British television - now headily enriched by Channel 4 experiment - the feature industry has struggled to find a model to intervene in the rip tides of the world market in cinema. Those attempts, too numerous, complex, and, in some ways, too sad, to enumerate, have foundered on the notion that large sums of public money can and should be deployed at government level to enable the UK industry to compete with the multinationally based Americans. It has never worked. By and large the world market looks after itself. If companies that dominate the world market - all American - think a film will make money and can be made economically in the UK, the film will be made. Global marketing power guarantees returns in the USA and elsewhere. Can Britain get into the act?

A lot of film-makers hope it can. Facing a Tory government teetering on the brink of abandoning what remains of public support for the film industry - Films Quota, Eady Levy, the Cinematograph Films Council - powerful voices - not least that of Alan Sapper - argued not simply for a radical new British Film Authority accountable to a single ministry, but for a transformed and interventionist Eady Levy raising tens of millions a year from levying blank video cassette sales and network television's heavy reliance on features. The claimants on any new fund already exist. Aspirant feature film-makers, the NFFC, the National Film School, the CFF, cinemas, training and cultural organisations.

One thing is apparent. While the industry can coalesce around the demand for a new funding base, there is a central argument - cultural, political and economic - about where and how the new income should be spent. That we need it is unarguable. How we spend it is fiercely controversial. Any policy narrowly confined to features and smartening up our commercial cinemas will be inadequate. The hammerlock of the American multinationals in cinema and television demands careful consideration.

The regional dimension

One response to this fault line in the economy of our movie industry has grown out of ACTT's new regional structure. Originally legitimised by Britain's growing population of film-makers outside the metropolitan and Home Counties heartland, the new regional sections bit the bullet of recruiting professional film-makers in the grant-aided and independent cultural sector. Their radicalism paid off. The sections injected a new energy into ACTT. For the first time the union focused on the work of those passionate but underfunded film workers who had no wish to work through the mainstream industry.

These developments have grown significantly. The initial Codes of Practice with the BFI and the Regional Arts Associations, were followed by the formation of a major London-based grant-aided film-makers section, and, finally, the crucial development of the union's Workshop Declaration, an unprecedented basis for permanent employment in cultural film work in annually funded, democratic units operating with full control over their work. Controlled access to television, allied to Channel 4, BFI, local authority and RAA funding, built a growing network of eleven committed workshops in less than a year.

The potential is enormous. For less than the budget of one smallish feature, a network of vigorous production units has emerged, with strong regional roots and functions ranging from exhibition and

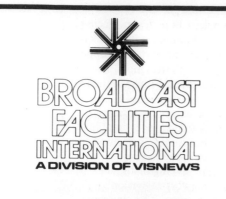

research, to education and production. With strong links with local labour movements and an abrasive radicalism, the workshops are the nearest any organisation has come to building a national film culture from the bottom up - breaking out of the erratic lottery of one-off productions. Strong links with other deeply concerned organisations figure in a union outreach that now embraces the Independent Film-makers' Association, the RAAs, elements of the BFI and local authorities.

The success of this new movement in production is beginning to spill into the cinema sector where independent distributors and exhibitors are looking hard at new forms of cinema to plug the haemorrhage of collapsing attendances and cinema closures. Fusing these ideas into a new strategy could mark out the siteplan for a lively new film culture, tightly related to the need for a collectivist response to the atomisation of the VCR and the home television screen. The unemployed, the old, black, brown, white, men and women, coming together in a new and radical art that just might change the nation we live in.

The challenges ahead

While technology is not neutral, it operates within the pounds and pence parameters of the dominant economic and social forces - imagination is indispensable in shaping the political structures in which technical change takes place. Here the union is both aggressive and defensive.

Cable television, scurried through in the Hunt Report's frantic haste to thrust monetarism into broadcasting, has been exposed as a hot air balloon of rhetoric. The wobbly suggestion that cable would lead to a production boom in the UK has fallen heavily to the ground. If - and it might be a big if - the cable consortia get off the ground, they will almost certainly buy their programming from the cheapest sources of mainstream programming. A smiling multinational Uncle Sam offers the obvious source of cheap audience-building programming - and mainstream it will have to be. The cable companies are brutally explicit - they don't want to make programmes in the UK.

Good original programming is expensive. The diversity and richness of the BBC, ITV and Channel 4 are economically sound because audiences of millions make the viewing hour cost astonishingly cheap.

Those economies of scale are what permits the dramas, current affairs, light entertainment, hard news, sport and education on UK television. That and public regulation which demands plurality and choice, even in peak-time, and controls, though some argue not sufficiently, the old movies and dog-eared repeats.

But if there is to be no public regulation, if the businessmen, frantically trying to pay off the vast charges on the millions their new cable networks will cost them, are then given a free hand, the implications for writers, actors, musicians and technicians in Britain may be serious. Added to the powerful arguments banged home by British Telecom that fibre optic cable and not potentially obsolete co-axial copper is the relevant technology, is the ominous threat to public service broadcasting.

Seriously accountable only to private businessmen, free to advertise and with few real restraints on programming, the Thatcherite cable model could erode the tradition of pluralist broadcasting in the BBC and ITV - more means worse.

The policies outlined in the Thatcher government's White Paper rule out the real potential of local cable services genuinely doing things that network TV can't. They would elbow aside the enthusiasm of Britain's great democratic regional authorities, elected and accountable, in favour of a broken backed 'regulatory' authority. Cable is too serious to leave to the market.

The potential is enormous for education, ethnic minorities, local community news services. None of this can make sense in an unco-ordinated national patchwork of market-dominated commercial services without the will or the means to do little more than show mainstream entertainment. Clearly ACTT - and every other broadcaster and politician - has the urgent responsibility of developing a new model which can begin to meet new social and democratic priorities. Economics and technology make that a difficult task, but ACTT cannot write off the challenge of cable television.

Shrewd as ever, the BBC believes that the only paying audience for additional TV services wants more feature films. Its satellite goes up in 1986. It will not be the last. All over Europe the race is on. National regulation has limited utility. Significantly, FISTAV, the powerful international organisation of film and TV unions, is designed to meet this challenge and is already active.

Such are the new challenges for the 1980s. A new marketism that seeks to abolish the historic recognition that film and broadcasting are a nation in dialogue with itself. A dialogue that requires attentive interest on the part of society if it is not to be colonised totally by the multinational broadcasting and film corporations.

GRANADA TELEVISION

FIFTY-UP

Now that the audience knows the whole story,
  Hearing of deeds we'd do well to recall,
Many, while raising their glasses, will wonder
  Just how the pioneers made the long haul.
Conquering mountains, their massive achievements
  Make Fitzcarraldo's appear bloody small.

Back in the heyday of Laughton and Korda
  Casual labour meant days without hope;
Oddballs attended the birth of the union
  (Captains don't come more courageous than Cope).
A lifeline from Elvin and Asquith to Sapper
  Calls for strong hands and more strands to the rope.

Time brings its changes, a shift of the focus,
  New opportunities mean bigger threats.
Cable and satellite offer rich pickings,
  Kicking an industry saddled with debts;
Zero-ing quotas and cancelling Eady –
  All with the Minister's 'deepest regrets'.

Free-for-all ventures mean freedom for vultures,
  Those who create should be seen and not heard.
Video makes the world safe for the pirates –
  Crisis in broadcasting? Don't be absurd.
Everything points to a brighter tomorrow,
  Even though Hunt is a four-letter word.

Fatal to kneel to the high priests of profit,
  Hearts made of concrete and heads made of wood;
Filled with a fervent concern for their pockets,
  They would lay everything waste if they could.
While they are pushing the mindless and shoddy,
  Others will fight to defend what is good.

Roger Woddis

GOLDCREST

— COMMITTED
TO QUALITY BRITISH
FEATURE FILMS
AND TELEVISION
PRODUCTIONS...

131-133 Holland Park Avenue, London W11 4UT.
Telephone: 01 602 6626. Telex: 267458 Goldcr.

KEY DATES

Why they joined

'There were two or three of us who got very annoyed because the people who owned the films and financed them, they used to take them and hack them about and that sort of thing. So, the directors of the period got together...and formed an association, which claimed the right to edit the first cut of their pictures. Out of this the Association of Cinematograph Technicians derived and I supported this for all I was worth. I was one of the people who insisted on being a member and I used to use the letters ACT after my name and all that sort of thing. This used to make me very unpopular with most of the employers, but I was sufficiently in demand not to care a damn, and I didn't and still don't'.

Maurice Elvey, director

'Although we were doing very well in 1933 on account of sound coming in, making the newsreel right up-to-date, and although the money was better, we worked night and day.' Alf Tunwell joined, but many of his highly individualistic colleagues refused to, having been 'bitten' once before by a previous abortive attempt to organise in which they had lost their subscription money. It was not until the war that the majority of his fellow newsreel workers joined ACT with him. Until then, however, the Newsreel Association was, happily, unaware of just how few ACT members there were in newsreels.

Alf Tunwell, newsreel cameraman

'My ACTT number is 461 but my original number was four or five as I first joined ACT in Shepherd's Bush Market in 1933 for 2/6d paid to a Captain Cope. I was then working at Gaumont-British, Lime Grove. In 1933 when we trooped around to Shepherd's Bush to join this new union we had heard about, we welcomed its instigation as we had always been working very hard; without proper breaks, night and day; very irregular, if any, meal breaks, often to the point of illness on many occasions. It bred a need for union control although there were only a few of us until the amount of members began to gather momentum up to the war in 1939, when most of us joined up, as I did, the RAF. Subsequently, on my return to the business in 1946, I was re-numbered 461 in the union'.

Ted Lloyd, cameraman

June 1933
The Association of Cine-Technicians is registered as a trade union.

January 1934
George Elvin appointed as General Secretary.

May 1935
First number published of the Journal of the Association of Cine-Technicians, now Film and TV Technician.

December 1936
First industrial agreement signed, with Gaumont-British Picture Corporation.
ACT affiliates to the Trades Union Congress.

May 1937
Anthony Asquith first elected as President.

April 1938
New Cinematograph Films Act.

February 1939
First major agreements signed with the laboratory section of the Film Production Employers' Federation (forerunner of the Film Laboratory Association).

1940
Campaign to incorporate film production into the government war effort.

1941
Service Film Units staffed with ACT members.

September 1942
First agreement with the Association of Specialised Film Producers.

January 1943
First agreement with the British Film Producers' Association.
Decision taken (by ballot) to affiliate to the Labour Party.

September 1944
First agreement with the Newsreel Association.

September 1945
National Arbitration Tribunal awards in favour of ACT following labs dispute.

March-April 1946
Repair and Despatch Strike.

June 1947
Demarcation Agreements signed between ACT, ETU and NATKE.

April 1948
New Cinematograph Films Act.

May 1950
Formation of ACT Films Ltd.

January 1951
Mass trade union demonstration at Wyndham's Theatre to focus government and public attention on the plight of British film industry.

February 1952
The end of an era. ACT fails to prevent government from abolishing the Crown Film Unit (formerly the GPO Film Unit).

November 1953
The beginning of an era. Parliament approves introduction of commercial television.

March 1954
Laboratory lock-out and strike.

April 1955
Strike to achieve ACT recognition in commercial television.

March 1956
ACT becomes ACTT, the Association of Cinematograph, Television and allied Technicians.

August 1957
Agreement signed with the Programme Contractors' Association on behalf of technicians employed in commercial television.

March 1959
First Annual Delegate Conference instead of Annual General Meeting.

October 1960
New shorts agreement between ACTT and the ASFP.

First ACTT weekend school organised.

February 1961
New television agreement signed between ACTT and the ITCA, operative until June 1964.

March 1961
Newsreel agreement signed between ACTT and Pathé News; British Movietonews.

June 1961
Increases gained to the scheduled minimum rates of the BFPA agreement after bitter dispute.

February 1963
Further increases gained to the scheduled minimum rates of the BFPA agreement.

March 1963
Redundancies at Westward Television.

July 1964
First national television strike.

Television agreement (three-year).

August 1965
Laboratory differentials agreement.

December 1965
Feature film agreement (three-year).

1966
First ACTT book published — *A Long Look at Short Films* by Vincent Porter and Derrick Knight.

May 1967
Reorganisation of BBC recruitment and recognition campaign.

June 1967
Television re-deployment following redistribution of ITV contracts.

August 1967
Shorts agreement.
AFLE agreement.

February 1968
Death of Anthony Asquith, ACTT President since 1937; the union co-operates in the establishment of a memorial fund.

March 1968
First ETV shop formed at the Council for English Teaching Overseas.

June 1968
ITA transmitter staff recruited.

August 1968
ITV dispute.

April 1969
Alan Sapper appointed as General Secretary.
George Elvin elected as President.

June 1969
New television agreement.

July 1969
AFLE agreement.

August 1969
AFLE agreement referred to the PIB (Prices and Incomes Board).

November 1969
PIB report on the AFLE agreement published; recommendation that implementation of settlement be subject to a standstill.

December 1969
DEP authorises implementation of AFLE settlement from February 1970.

February 1970
ACTT takes Kodak to industrial court.

April 1970
Annual Conference confirms appointment of Alan Sapper as General Secretary.

May 1970
Industrial court awards in favour of ACTT in Kodak dispute.

June 1970
Granada TV strike.

June 1970
MGM studios close.

July 1970
Intensive campaign to reverse closure decision at MGM.

April 1971
New agreement with FSFA for shorts and documentary films.

July 1971
New agreement with AFLE for laboratory members.

April 1972
TV Commission report published.

August 1972
New feature film agreement.

April 1973

George Elvin resigns as President of ACTT and retires.

Sidney Cole elected as President.

Independent Local Radio Section set up.

August 1973

Report of the film nationalisation forum published.

September 1973

ACTT wins COI dispute after a prolonged struggle.

1975

Patterns of Discrimination published.

New Cinematograph Films Act from which the National Film Development Fund emerged.

1976

Sidney Cole retires.

Robert Bolt elected as President.

1978

Strike at Granada TV.

1979

Abortive attempt at amalgamation with the ABS.

ITV strike.

Ron Bowey elected as President.

1980

Capital Radio strike.

January 1981

First ACTT Women's Conference.

1982

Dennis Claridge becomes President on resignation of Ron Bowey.

Union's first Equality Officer takes up post.

House of Lords finds for union in Hadmor case.

Workshop Declaration for the grant-aided film sector.

Video (non-broadcast) Section of ACTT set up.

Channel 4 begins.

1983

Breakfast television launched.

ACTT Rules Revision Conference approves new divisional structure to increase democratic participation.

Affiliation agreement signed by ACTT with Directors Guild of America and Directors Guild of Canada.

Bruce Anderson elected as President of ACTT.

MEMBERSHIP STATISTICS

Year	Total
1933	98

Officially, ie notwithstanding Captain Cope's possible recruitment of many more who may have paid one subscription and then lapsed.

Year	Total
1934	88
1935	605
1936	1,122
1937	1,289
1938	1,212
1939	915

Reflects early war crisis before official war-time film units were established and when many members left to join the Armed Forces or engaged in other forms of National Service.

Year	Total	Women
1940	1,053	112
1941	1,936	416
1942	2,908	861
1943	3,744	1,147
1944	4,302	1,375
1945	5,168	1,356
1946	6,460	1,662
1947	7,507	1,769
1948	7,788	1,665
1949	7,556	1,517
1950	7,819	1,553
1951	5,422	925
1952	5,566	967
1953	5,830	1,027
1954	6,092	1,099

Year	Total	Women
1955	6,734	1,207
1956	7,269	1,305
1957	8,067	1,474
1958	7,497	1,517
1959	8,149	1,612
1960	9,125	1,789
1961	10,410	2,002
1962	11,637	2,232
1963	12,271	2,282
1964	12,114	No record
1965	12,723	2,128
1966	11,503	1,955
1967	12,683	2,008
1968	14,077	1,536
1969	15,827	1,836
1970	16,545	2,209
1971	17,183	2,308
1972	18,517	2,651
1973	18,458	2,739
1974	18,690	2,871
1975	19,460	3,128
1976	18,682	3,074
1977	19,974	3,427
1978	20,540	3,656
1979	21,712	4,099
1980	20,011	3,912
1981	20,021	4,018
1982	21,012	4,354

Note: From time to time, eg 1980, grand totals of union membership decreased as a result of records overhauls. It should be obvious, however, that these periodic recalculations in no way affect the fairly steady rise in membership over the decades.

175

INDEX